Jeffrey Gitomer's

LITTLE RED BOOK
of SELLING

+≡ 12.5 Principles ≡+
of Sales Greatness

How to make sales FOREVER

Bard Press
Austin

The Little Red Book of Selling

Copyright © 2005 by Jeffrey Gitomer

The Little Red Book of Selling is a registered trademark of Jeffrey Gitomer.

To order additional copies of this title,
contact your local bookstore or call 704.333.1112.
The author may be contacted at the following address:
BuyGitomer
310 Arlington Avenue, Loft 329
Charlotte, NC 28203
Phone 704.333.1112, fax 704.333.1011
E-mail: salesman@gitomer.com
Web sites: www.gitomer.com, www.trainone.com

Cover Graphic by Dave Pinksi.
Cover Design by Mike Sakoonserksadee.
Photography by Mitchell Kearney.
Page design by Greg Russell.

Printed in China by R.R. Donnelley.

Box set edition, ctober 2007

Library of Congress Cataloging-in-Publication Data

Gitomer, Jeffrey H.
    Jeffrey Gitomer's little red book of selling : the 12.5 principles of
    sales greatness: how to make sales forever / Jeffrey Gitomer
    p. cm
    ISBN 1-885167-60-1 (cloth)
    ISBN 978-1-885167-60-6
    1 Selling. 2. Business networks. 3. Customer loyalty.
    4. Customer relations. II. Title

HF5438.25 G58 2004
658.85--dc22   S/B I.Author
                                                    2003070815

If they like you,
and they believe you,
and they trust you,
and they have
confidence in you …
then they *MAY*
buy from you.

– Jeffrey Gitomer

People don't like
to be sold …

… but they love to buy!

"Why They Buy"
An answer every salesperson needs.

"Why do people buy?" is a thousand times more important than "How do I sell?" No, let me correct that … it's one million times more important than "How do I sell?" No, let me correct that … it's one billion times more important than "How do I sell?" Get the picture?

I have just spent three days in our studio interviewing the customers of my customers, asking them "why they buy." And the answers are a combination of common sense, startling information, overlooked issues, and incredible opportunity.

It never ceases to amaze me that companies will spend thousands of hours and millions of dollars teaching people "how to sell," and not one minute or not ten dollars on "why they buy." And "why they buy" is all that matters.

You may think you know why they buy, but you probably don't do anything about it. Proof? Let me share with you the early warning signals that prove you may not have a clue as to why they buy.

1. **You get price objections.**

2. **You have to send bids or proposals.**

3. **They claim to be satisfied with their present supplier.**

4. **No one will return your call.**

4.5 **You are complaining that the economy is slow.**

If these sound familiar to you, you may be in the big club.

I am going to present a collection of elements as to why customers buy. They are in no particular order, but they are valid reasons, which were given to me straight from the mouths of customers, from every type of business.

1. I like my sales rep.

NOTE WELL: Liking is the single most powerful element in a sales relationship. I got a quote the other day from someone claiming to be a sales expert. It started out saying, "Your customer does not have to like you, but he does have to trust you." What an idiot. Can you imagine the CEO of the company, when making a buying decision, saying, "I trusted that guy, but I sure didn't like him." Like leads to trust. Trust leads to buying. Buying leads to relationship. That's not the life cycle, that's the life cycle of sales.

2. I understand what I am buying.

3. I perceive a difference in the person and the company that I am buying from.

4. I perceive a value in the product that I am purchasing.

5. I believe my sales rep.

6. I have confidence in my sales rep.

7. I trust my sales rep.

8. I am comfortable with my sales rep.

9. I feel that there is a fit of my needs and his/her product or service.

10. The price seems fair, but it's not necessarily the lowest.

11. I perceive that this product or service will increase my productivity.

12. I perceive that this product or service will increase my profit.

12.5 I perceive that my salesperson is trying to help me build my business in order to earn his. My salesperson is a valuable resource to me.

Well, there are a few reasons to get your thought process going. If you discover yours, selling will be a snap.
Go, do, now!

"Jeffrey," you whine, "Tell me how!"

OK, Here's what to do.

1. Call six of your best customers.

2. Invite them to a seminar about how to build THEIR business

3. Offer GREAT food.

4. Tell them that there are also 15-20 minutes worth of questions you want to ask them about how to strengthen your relationship.

5. Craft six questions about how you meet their needs and what they look for in a vendor/partner.

6. RECORD the session. Video is best, but audio will do. Then listen to the recording 100 times.

I have given you some answers as to why customers buy.
But the bigger question is: Why do YOUR customers buy?
Think you know? Want a cold slap in the face?
YOU'VE NEVER EVEN ASKED THEM!

It amazes me that this answer is so obvious, yet so overlooked.

Free Red✗Bit: Want a list of "why they buy" questions
to ask? I've compiled a list of a few questions that will get
the session started. Go to www.gitomer.com, register if you are
a first time user, and enter WHY THEY BUY in the RedBit box.

Selling is puking.
Your customer wants to buy.

Got a hot prospect list?
Hot for who?
How many are hot for you?
I'll bet that's a (way) smaller list.

The Little RED Book of Selling
Table of Contents

Understanding *Red* Sales...

The 12.5 *Red* Principles of Sales Greatness:

More RED SALES Thinking
Strategies at the end to help you win at the beginning

Selling in the Red Zone

I'm not just an expert in sales. I'm a salesperson who has made millions of dollars worth of sales, and has remained a student of sales. And besides, who just wants to be AN expert when you can be THE expert?

In this *Little Red Book of Selling*, you will have the opportunity to understand why sales happen. And by mastering the elements that I give you, make sales happen for yourself – forever. The difference between success and mediocrity is **philosophy**. Most salespeople think end of the month. But you have to begin thinking *end of time*. That's how I think.

If you think end of time, each time you are in a selling situation, the sale will always be long term, relationship driven, and referral oriented. And it has nothing to do with sales manipulation, or other seedy tactics. That has given real salespeople a bad rep.

The Little Red Book of Selling could also be titled the *Little Red Book of Buying*. The subtle difference in sales between the successful and the unsuccessful is the difference between trying to sell what you have and creating the atmosphere where the prospect will buy what you have. *People don't like to be sold, but they love to buy* has become more than a registered trademark to me – it's my mantra. And throughout the course of this book you must begin to adopt a philosophy that drives you to a higher, value driven, helping purpose.

OK, I know. It sounds like a college professor. It even sounds unrealistic on the surface. But keep in mind I was raised in New Jersey, went to college in Philadelphia, had businesses in the Philadelphia metropolitan area, and sold garments in Manhattan for five years – successfully – without giving one bribe (even though EVERYONE either expected one or asked for one).

In all of my sales battles both victorious and in utter defeat, I have learned millions of dollars worth of lessons that you will be receiving in this Red Book for somewhere around $20.

Instead of thinking *end of month*, begin thinking *end of time*.

Here's how to take the
golden information inside
The Little Red Book of Selling
and transfer it into your sales success.

I will give the gold to you
in **bite size** chunks.

You can **absorb the nuggets**
anywhere, at any time.

You can **try them out**
the same moment
you learn them.

There will also be every imaginable ancillary product to help
you further your understanding of sales and why people buy.
You can get additional CDs, flashcards, streaming video on
the Internet, you name it, to help you understand, implement,
and execute the most powerful selling strategies that I know.

If you can't use these strategies to build your success, it is my
highest recommendation that you get out of sales as fast as
you can.

If you master them and implement one skill per day into your
life, and your sales life, at the end of one year you will be an
expert. An expert with a bigger bank account.

Note to readers: This book contains language used by real people used in real situations in sales. I have not edited this book for political correctness, (I am a male. I tend to speak in the male gender), nor have I edited it for real world selling situations that I face every day.

I have edited out one thing, all the bullshit.

If any of this is offensive to you, get out of sales as fast as you can and take a nice safe job with some big company where you can whine all day, and complain about your low pay.

But if you want to be the sales success that you dream about, and in the end be fulfilled because you did it "your way," then this is a book to be purchased immediately, read twice, studied, implemented as fast as you can, and referred to every day.

If you want to have your cake and eat it too, then I guarantee this book is for you.

Jeffrey Gitomer

Turn the page …

The Little RED Book of Selling is NOT just about how to make a sale. It's about how to make sales FOREVER!

How to read this book.

How to implement these principles.

How to use the principles of this book to succeed!

This book is *RED*. Emphasis will be placed in key areas and you'll know them because they're red. But understand that it's about every word, not just the red words.

This book must be *READ*. In order for you to get the most out of this book, you must actually read each word. I have taken great pains to eliminate all fluff. What you'll find in here is all red meat.

This book must be *RE-READ*. As you face your real world selling, you will find applications for each of these principles. I made the book small, so you can carry it with you and use the principles, as they're called for, in every selling situation you face. The more you carry the book, the more sales you will make.

This book is *MARGINAL*. In the margins you'll find every "sales whine," which we refer to as red whines, you've ever uttered. And maybe even some you didn't know existed. The good news is that I've answered every one of them. When you're finished reading this book the words "quit your whining" will never have to be uttered to you again.

Look out for the *RED BITES*. At the end of each principle are several information bites that will help you understand the principle in a way that you can use it.

Go get the *RED BIT*. Additional valuable information is available on my website www.gitomer.com. I put it there so that you would actually have to take an action on your own behalf. There's more red gold on my website. All you have to do is go there and mine it. It's free.

This book is *MONEY*. Your money. As you study these principles, your sales will increase. As you implement these principles, your sales will begin to take off. As you master these principles, your sales will skyrocket.

Turn the page.

Why is this book RED?

RED is the color of *passion*.

Passion is the fulcrum point of selling.
No passion, no sales.

RED is the color of *love*.

If you don't love what you sell,
go sell something else.

RED is the *brightest* color.

You must be bright in order
to convert selling to buying.

RED is the most *visible* color.

You must be visible to your customers
with a value message, not just a sales pitch.

And RED is *fire*.

If you're not on fire, you'll lose
to someone who is.

All of these attributes of **RED** must be present in a salesperson
as a basic fundamental of success. If you don't love it, if you ain't
passionate about it, if you ain't on fire, you're gonna lose the sale
to someone who is. The Little Red Book of Selling is **RED** for a
reason: It's not just the principles, it's not just the **RED** bites, it's
not just the **RED** bits, it's not just the **RED** whines; it's the love
of what you do. Your passion for excellence will lead you to the
mastery of the Little Red Principles of Selling.

What's the best way to read this book? **Slowly.**
What's the best way to master each of these principles?
One at a time.

1. Read each page twice. Once to "get" the idea. Twice to
understand the idea.

2. Think about how each principle or thought applies to you.
How you live, how you think, how you act, how you react,
and how you sell.

3. Study and implement an application. One of the secrets
to becoming great at selling is to apply and implement
techniques and strategies as they are learned. Reading it
is worthless unless you apply it.

4. Pick up the phone and try it. The sooner you try to apply
what you have learned, the faster it will become part of
your own mastery process.

4.5 Don't whine if it doesn't work right away. And don't be
blaming me. Not only do these principles work, they work
in the Northeast, where people eat their young.

♥ Here's the secret. Be your own valentine. You can find
this secret in the colored illustration as soon as you open the
book. Look for the little red heart. See it? As you are climbing
the ladder of success you have to put your heart into your
work, and you have to love what you do. On the surface,
it doesn't seem like much of a secret, but I promise you it's
the difference between going up the ladder and going down
the ladder.

What's the difference between failure and success in salespeople?

What does it take to become a sales success?

I wanna be a success! I wanna be a success!

There is no quick fix, magic wand, or potion that will give you the success you're dreaming for. So, what's the secret of sales success? Well – it's not a single secret – it's a secret formula. There is a series of 18.5 principles, strategies, and actions that will lead you to success.

OK, OK, the *Secrets of Sales Success* are not real secrets, they're fundamental steps that successful salespeople and entrepreneurs have been executing for centuries. These are attributes that high achievers have in common. *Here are the 18.5 Secrets of Success: (And more important, are you a master of each of these characteristics?)*

1. Believe you can. Have the mental posture for success. Believe you are capable of achieving it. This belief must extend to their product and their company. A strong belief system seems obvious – but few people possess it. Too many salespeople look outside (for the money they can make) rather than look inside (for the money they can earn). Believing that you're the best and that believing you're capable of achievement is the hardest thing to do. It requires daily dedication to self-support, self-encouragement and positive self-talk. *How much do you believe in you?*

2. Create the environment. The right home and work environment will encourage you. Supportive spouse, family members, and co-workers will make the road to success a smooth ride. It's up to you to create it. *How conducive is your environment to attitude and success?*

3. Have the right associations. Hang around the right people. Other successful people. Network where their best customers and prospects go. Join the right associations. Make the right friends. Stay away from poison people – the one's who can't seem to get anywhere. Have a mentor or three. Who do you hang around with? That is who you are likely to become. *How successful are the people you associate with?*

4. Expose yourself to what's new. If you're not learning every day – your competition is. New information is essential to success (unless you're like most salespeople who already know everything - lucky you). *How much time are you spending each day learning something new?*

5. Plan for the day. Since you don't know on which day success will occur, you'd better be ready every day. Prepare with education. Plan with goals, and the details for their achievement. Learning and goals are the surest methods to be ready for your success. *Are your plans and goals in front of your face every day?*

6. Become valuable. The more valuable you become, the more the marketplace will reward you. Give first. Become known as a resource, not a salesperson. Your value is linked to your knowledge and your willingness to help others. *How valuable are you to others?*

7. Have the answers your prospects and customers need. The more you can solve problems, the easier path you will have to sales success. Prospects don't want facts, they want answers. In order to have those answers, you must have superior knowledge about what you do – and explain it in terms of how the prospect uses what you do. *How good are your answers?*

8. Recognize opportunity. Stay alert for the situations that can create success opportunities. The little known key is to get and maintain a positive attitude. Attitude allows you to see the possibilities when opportunity strikes – because it often shows up in the form of adversity. *How well do you spot opportunity?*

9. Take advantage of opportunity. First, recognize it (often it shows up disguised in the form of adversity). Second, act on it. Opportunity is elusive. It exists all over the place, but very few can see it. Some people fear it because it involves change; most don't believe they are capable of achievement. *Do you seize opportunity?*

10. Take responsibility. We all blame others to a degree. Blame is tied to success in reverse proportion. The lower your degree of blame – the higher degree of success you'll achieve. Get the job done yourself no matter what. Petty blame is rampant and the biggest waste of time. Don't blame others or yourself. Take responsibility for your actions and decisions. Blaming others is an easy thing to do, but leads to a path of mediocrity. Successful people take responsibility for everything they do AND everything that happens to them. *Do you blame or take responsibility for your actions?*

11. Take action. Just do it (Nike) was the expression for the '90s. Actions are the only way to bridge plans and goals with accomplishment. Nothing happens until you do something to make it happen – every day. *Are you action or B.T.N.A. (big talk, no action)?*

12. Make mistakes. The best teacher is failure. It's the rudest of awakenings, and the breeding ground for self-determination. Don't think of them as mistakes – think of them as learning experiences not to be repeated. *How willing are you to make mistakes?*

13. Willing to risk. This is the most crucial factor. No risk, no reward is the biggest understatement in the business world. It should be stated – no risk, no nothing. Taking chances is a common thread among every successful person. No risk, no reward the saying goes – and it's true. Most people won't risk because they think they fear the unknown. The real reason people won't risk is that they lack the preparation and education that breeds the self-confidence (self-belief) to take a chance. Risk is the basis of success. If you want to succeed, you'd better be willing to risk whatever it takes to get there. *How willing are you to risk?*

14. Keep your eyes on the prize. Post your goals. Stay focused on your dreams and they will become reality. Too many foolish diversions will take you off the path. *How focused is your success effort? As focused as your play effort?*

15. Balance yourself. Your physical, spiritual and emotional health are vital to your success quest. Plan your time to allow your personal goals to be synergized with your work goals. *How balanced are you?*

16. Invest, don't spend. There should be a 10-20% gap between earning and spending. Clip your credit cards in half and make a few investments – with professional guidance. *Do you invest (in yourself) each month?*

17. Stick at it until you win. Most people fail because they quit too soon. Don't let that be you. Make a plan AND a commitment to see the plan through – no matter what. Don't quit on the ten yard line. Have whatever it takes to score. *How many projects do you abandon before they're complete?*

18. Develop and maintain a positive attitude. Surprisingly this is not a common characteristic. By the time many make it to the top, they have developed irreversible cynicism. But positive attitude makes achieving success much easier – and more fun. *How positive is your attitude?*

18.5 Ignore idiots and zealots. Also known as pukers, these people will try to rain on your parade (discourage you) because they have no parade of their own. Avoid them at all costs.

See, I told you – no revelations. OK, so if these characteristics seem so simple, how come they're so difficult to master? Answer – your lack of personal self-discipline and a dedication to life-long learning. Oh yeah, that.

I am consistently amazed and disappointed at the small number of people willing to execute the simple daily self-disciplines needed to reach higher levels of success. They know it will bring them the success they dream about, yet they fail to execute.

In sales, or any business effort, or career position, the person who will emerge victorious most of the time, is the person who wants it the most. Victory does not always go to the swift (hare vs. tortoise), victory does not always go to the powerful (David vs. Goliath), and victory does not always go to the lowest price (Yugo vs. Mercedes).

The victory we call success goes to the best prepared, self believing, right associated, self taught, responsible person, who sees the opportunity and is willing to take a risk to seize it – sometimes a big risk. Is that you?

There's the secret – and it's not real complicated. It's not nuclear physics or brain surgery. And now that I've shared it with thousands of people, you'd think there would be a surge in the ratio of successful salespeople. Nope.

The reason the success formula is considered a secret is that it remains an enigma. It seems that there are very few people who are willing to put forth the *effort* to get from where they are to where they want to be. Most make excuses and blame others for their own poor choices.

The biggest secret (and the biggest obstacle) to success is you. The formula is there for everyone to know – BUT, there's a big difference in knowing what to do, and doing it.

Now that you know the difference, why will some of you still fail? The answers are inside this book. But as my friend Harvey Mackay says, "Don't read this book. Study it!"

What is your biggest fear -- speaking, rejection, or failing?

It is said that speaking in public (making a presentation to a group) is a bigger fear than death. I don't buy it. I think if someone put a gun to your head and said speak in public or die – you'd find that lost William Jennings Bryan oration within you.

Many salespeople fear making sales presentations. But, by far, the biggest fear salespeople have is fear of failure. It has a cousin – fear of rejection. Rejection is the pathway to failure – if you fear it. While failure itself is real, the fear of it is a condition of the mind.

Earl Nightingale's legendary tape "The Strangest Secret" says, "You become what you think about." If that's true, why doesn't everyone think "success"? The answer is a combination of what we expose ourselves to, and how we condition ourselves.

We live in a world of negative conditioning. The three big motivators are … fear, greed, and vanity. They drive the American sales process – and they drive the American salesperson.

Our society preys on the fear factor. It's in 50% of the ads we see (the rest are greed or vanity). Ads about life insurance for death and disability, stolen credit cards, anti-freeze for stalled cars, tires that grip the road in the rain, brakes that stop to avoid hitting a child on a bike, and security systems so your home won't be robbed. If you see that crap enough, you become "fear-conditioned."

We are constantly reminded to carry mace, get a burglar alarm, and be sure we have The Club. To make matters worse we now see police at ATM machines, metal detectors in schools, and can rely on the local news to promulgate the trend. They are dedicated to promote issues of fear every minute they're on the air.

Once society gives you fear, it's natural that you take it with you into the workplace. It transmutes into a fear of failure. This fear intensifies in workplaces with hostile environments. Bosses and managers who threaten, intimidate and ridicule.

In the midst of this we struggle for success. And while we think we fear failure, or at least don't want it around us – we all face it in one form or another every day. Everyone fails. But, failure is relative. Its measurement is subjective. Mostly it occurs in your mind. If you exchange "I failed" for "I learned what never to do again," it's a completely different mindset. The status of failure is up to you.

Over the years of my failures, I have developed a great way of looking at it (lots of practice). I learn from it, or I ignore it.

Thomas Edison – failed 6,000 times before the light bulb,
Donald Trump had monumental failures on his way to the top,
Mike Schmidt – third baseman for the Philadelphia Phillies,
failed at the plate (at bat) two out of three times for 20 years,
and was inducted into baseball's hall of fame as one of the
greatest ball players of all time. Were these men failures?
Did they fear failure?

There are degrees of failure in sales.
Here are some external ones:

- **Failure to prepare**
- **Failure to make contacts**
- **Failure to make a sale**
- **Failure to meet a quota**
- **Failure to keep a job**

External (outside) fears lead to internal (inside) fears – fear
based on what happens when you fail or are close to failing.
Your reaction to internal fear determines your fate. It's not
what happens to you, it's what you do with what happens to
you. *Here are the five typical reactions to rejection or failure:*

1. **Curse it.**
2. **Deny it (a nice way of saying lie about it).**
3. **Avoid it.**
4. **Make an excuse about it.**
5. **Blame others (the easiest thing to do).**
6. **Quit.**

Failure actually only occurs when you decide to quit. You choose your results. *Here are a few simple things you can do to avoid getting to the "quit" stage:*

- **Look at failure as an event, not a person.**
- **Look for the why, and find the solution (If you look at "no" hard enough, it will lead you to yes).**
- **List possible opportunities.**
- **Ask yourself, what have I learned? And try again.**
- **Don't mope around with other failures -- go find a successful person, and hang around him.**

Here are a few complicated things you can do to avoid getting to the "I quit" stage:

- **Create a new environment.**
- **Cultivate new associations.**
- **Access new information.**
- **Get a new mind set -- create new background thoughts.**

It's always too soon to quit.

Afraid to speak, or afraid to fail? Which is the greater fear? When you consider the complications and ramifications of failure, making a speech to 1,000 people, by comparison, is a walk in the park.

The information is here.
The challenge has been laid down.
The rest is up to you.
I can bring you to the water,
but I can't push
your face down in it.
You have to drink it
one glass at a time.
And in the end,
the water will convert
to the finest champagne.
And, instead of drinking it,
you can toast yourself,
and just sip a glass of success.

The 12.5 Principles
of Sales Greatness

How to Make Sales
Forever

Principle 1

KICK YOUR OWN ASS

- The kick your own ass philosophy.
- Help I'm slumping and I can't make a sale.

Red Bites

- Bad day or bad attitude?
- Philosophy drives attitude.
- Develop a YES! Attitude.
- Celebrate effort, not victory.
- You know what to do, you just don't do it.
- Time management -- what's important now?
- Be selfish. Learn for yourself. Do it for yourself. Selfish wins.

"IT'S A MOTIVATIONAL TOOL I INVENTED. IT'S SORT OF LIKE
THE CARROT AND THE STICK, ONLY MORE EFFECTIVE."

Kick your own ass!

Ever have a bad day? Ever lose a sale you thought you had?

Ever been in a slump? Ever been rejected 10 straight times? Ever had someone say yes to you and three days later just evaporate? Can't get them on the phone? Won't call you back?

How do you react and respond to these situations?

Do you have all the sales training you need? Do you watch TV at night when you should be reading sales books or getting ready for your sales call the next day? Do you "party" at times when you really shouldn't? Do you get to work "on time" rather than make a sales call and a sale in the morning?

These are all symptoms. Not problems. They are symptoms of the fact that you are not self-motivated. That you are not self-starting. That you are not sales responsible. And that you are looking at your position as a job, not as a career.

Wanna know what to do about it? Wanna know the surefire way of making certain that you achieve the success, the money, the fulfillment and the personal gratification that comes with a sales career?

Here's the answer …

Kick your own ass!

No one will do it for you. No one really wants to help you. Very few will inspire you. And even fewer will care about you. People care about themselves. Just like you do.

Salespeople (not you of course) tend to whine. Slow sales, unreturned calls, competition undercutting, the usual. The same things they've been whining about for a hundred years. If you want an insurance policy for success in the profession of selling, you better issue it to yourself, pay for it yourself, name yourself as the policy holder, and down at the bottom, name yourself the beneficiary. Then have the balls to sign the document, and make a commitment to yourself.

RED WHINE ...

"They won't provide me any training."

Don't whine to me that your boss is a jerk. Get a new boss. Don't whine to me that the customer won't return your call. Study voicemail. Don't whine to me that your company won't give you a laptop. They sell them at the computer store. Go buy one.

Take a moment right now and look at your sales resource library. What kind of books do you have, what kind of tapes do you have on the subjects of selling, presentation skills, positive attitude, creativity, and humor that you read and refer to every day? Let me give you the answer. Not enough.

Regardless of your selling circumstance. Regardless of your success to this point in time. Regardless of your company. Regardless of your boss. You have a responsibility to yourself to achieve. Achieve a level of success that you set for yourself. Not a quota. Quotas to me are a bunch of crap set by management who couldn't go out and meet those quotas themselves if their lives depended on it. If you are a great salesperson you should meet your quota in the first two weeks of the month, and begin to bank real money the last two weeks. You should have your manager coming up to you to find out how you do it. You should have the president of the company calling you on the phone congratulating you on your successes.

RED SELLING RESPONSE ...

"Train yourself."

But let me give you a big clue. The only way this is going to happen is with self-inspiration, self-determination, and hard work that starts before everyone else gets up and after everyone else has gone to sleep. Kick your own ass is not a statement. It's an axiom.

An unbreakable rule that each salesperson, you included, must follow everyday. As fast as you can come to the understanding and realization that no one is going to hand you any degree of success. That's something you hand to yourself. Twenty-five years ago I was standing outside my hotel in Chicago waiting for Mel Green, the CEO of Advance Process Supply (my client). It was February. The snow was coming down sideways. It was 5:30 a.m. After I unthawed in the car, Mel and I began talking about his latest project which as usual turned from an idea into gold. "Damn you're lucky," I said. He looked at me and winked. "Hard work makes luck," he replied.

RED WHINE ...

"They won't buy me a laptop."

That single expression has been my gateway to millions of dollars. And it can be yours.

Not every human being agrees with my personality, my philosophies, or my style, but no human being can say that I don't work my ass off.

Chief Whiner

The secret I have found in the kick your own ass axiom is that most salespeople will not do the hard work that it takes to make selling easy.

But here's the bigger secret: work your ass off. All the rest of the principles can be taken to the highest level by working your ass off. Working your ass off leads to selling your ass off, and selling your ass off leads to banking your ass off.

Free Red **Bit**: Want my library list of recommended reading? Go to www.gitomer.com, register if you are a first time user, and enter the words SALES PILLS in the RedBit box. AND, as part of my commitment to you, I am offering you one free online training lesson. Just go to www.trainone.com, and click on the free demo. BUT you must have high speed Internet access to view. If you don't have it, you are losing to others that do.

RED SELLING RESPONSE ...

"Laptops are for sale at the computer store."

Invest in yourself.
Buy your own laptop.

Help! I'm slumping, and I can't get a sale!

In a slump? Not making enough (or any) sales. Feel like you're unable to get out of the rut? Is it the economy or is it YOU?

Maybe you're not in a big slump, but just can't seem to hit the quota numbers. Let's be kind and call it "sales underachievement."

Don't panic.

Don't press too hard.

Don't get down on yourself.

Don't get mad.

And above all – don't quit.

RED WHINE ...

"My boss won't motivate me."

OK, OK, there's a bit of a slowdown, but don't be too quick to blame your lack of performance on "it" before you take a hard look at "you."

Take a closer look at "slump" before you blame "economy." Here are the prime causes of sales slumps:

Poor belief system *I don't believe that my company or product is the best. I don't think that I'm the best.*

Poor work habits *Getting to work late, or barely "on time." Not spending your time with people who can say "yes."*

Misperceptions that lead to sour grapes *I think my prices are too high, or my territory is bad.*

Outside pressure *Caused by money problems, family problems, or personal problems.*

Poor personal habits *Too much drink, too much food, or too much after hours play.*

Boss giving crap instead of support *Someone who says, "You better do it," instead of, "I know you can do it."*

Events that go against you *New salesperson passes you, someone else gets promoted and you knew it should have been you.*

Customer cancels a big order *Weakening your personal belief or causing severe money problems – or both.*

Getting depressed *From any of the above.*

RED SELLING RESPONSE ...

"Motivate yourself."

When you're in a slump, you begin to press for orders instead of working your best gameplan (which is: "sell to help the other person," and let your sincerity of purpose shine through). When you have the pressure to sell, the prospect senses it, and backs off.

Then things get worse. You can't seem to sell at all, and begin to panic. Oh my gosh, I can't sell a thing, I'll get fired, miss my house payment, can't pay my bills – Aaaahhhhhh! False fear. Relax, you're better than that.

What causes a slump? You do. Therefore, you are the best (only) person to fix it. Here's a prescription to help cure sick sales:

• **Study basics** – Usually what's wrong is not complicated. In fact, you probably know what's wrong. Your problem is that you think it's someone or something else's fault. Wrong. List two or three areas that need immediate care. Have the guts to take action.

• **Revisit your (or make a new) plan for success** – Today.

• **List 5 things you could be doing to work smarter AND harder** – Make a plan to work as smart as you think (or say) you are. Hard work can change your luck.

• **Change your presentation** – Try a different approach. Take the customer's perspective.

• **Talk to your five best customers** – Ask them to evaluate your situation.

• **Get someone you respect to evaluate your presentation** – take them with you on sales calls. Get a coach.

- **Visit your mentor** – And have a new plan to discuss when you get there.

- **Get to work an hour before everyone** – Put in more productive time.

- **Stay away from pity parties** – Don't make a slump worse by whining or hanging around a bunch of negits and underachievers.

- **Hang around positive, successful people** – The best way to get to success.

- **Have some fun** – Go to the comedy club, do a little extra of what you like to do best (unless too much fun is the cause of your slump).

- **Spend 30 minutes a day (in the morning is best) reading about your positive attitude** – Then listen to attitude tapes and sales tapes in the car ALL DAY.

- **Listen to your favorite song just before the presentation** – Go in to your next call singing.

- **Take a day off** – Chill out, take stock, make a plan, re-group, re-energize, and return with renewed determination and better energy.

- **Rearrange your office** – Shake things up a little, make them look new.

- **Audiotape your presentations live** – Then listen in the car immediately afterwards. Take notes. Act to correct.

- **Videotape your presentation** – Watch it with others who can give you constructive feedback.

- **Take the best salesperson you know out on calls with you for a day** – Get a written evaluation after each call.

• **Take your boss with you on calls for a week** –
You'll get more feedback than you can handle, but it will help.

• **Avoid negative talk and negative people like the
plague** – Find people who will encourage you, not puke
on you.

When a baseball player is in a batting slump he will do
anything to "change his luck." Things from superstition
(rabbits foot, not shaving, wearing the same underwear) to
changing batting stance, to watching video, to extra coaching.
But the one thing that usually breaks the slump is extra batting
practice – to regain the groove. Fundamentals, baby.

They, like you, have the professional ability, but temporarily
lost it. They, like you, went back to the raw fundamentals to
regain lost talent.

Other random notes on the truth about slumps: The best
way to get out of the rut is keep the slump in perspective.
Once you accept the fact that you can change it, you can
begin to recover. Be cool – you're the greatest, if you think you
are. Believe in the most important person in the world – you.

In a sales slump?
Get fired up or get fired.

Red✶Bit of Free Inspiration: A famous (but author
unknown) poem "Don't Quit" is yours for the taking. A bit of
inspiration to egg you on. Go to www.gitomer.com, register if
you are a first time user, and enter the words DON'T QUIT in
the RedBit box.

Red Bites

Bad day or bad attitude? People always blame their attitude on the day. I'm having a bad day is baloney. What you're really saying is: I've let other people get to my attitude, I've let other circumstances get to my attitude. That's not only unjustifiable, it's a sign of mental weakness. If you tell yourself you're having a bad day, I promise you will have one, and if you tell yourself you're having a great day, I promise you will have one. The day is not bad unless you name it bad.

Philosophy drives attitude. "Attitude drives actions. Actions drive results. Results drive lifestyles." That's a quote from America's business philosopher, Jim Rohn. If you don't like your lifestyle, look at your results. If you don't like your results, look at your actions. If you don't like your actions, look at your attitude. If you don't like your attitude, look at your philosophy.

> ## Most salespeople make the fatal mistake of starting in the middle. They start with "action."

If you have no philosophy and you have a lousy attitude, what kind of actions are you going to take? And if I asked you right now what is your philosophy, you probably would respond, "duh!" If you would like a copy of my sales and life philosophy, go to www.gitomer.com and enter the word PHILOSOPHY in the RedBit box.

Develop a YES! Attitude. There is a subtle difference between a "positive" attitude and a "yes" attitude. Both are GREAT, but "yes" is a bit more powerful, because it assumes that everything will start with "yes," even when it's "no." A "yes" attitude helps you formulate the response in positive form. A "yes" attitude is more declarative. It tells people in a word that their expectations will be met, and somehow your answer to whatever they want or need will be "yes," or in a positive format. Everyone wants to hear "yes," and if you think of yourself as a "yes" person, not only will you be in a positive frame of mind but you will also have positive expectations.

Celebrate effort, not victory. Too many times salespeople and their leaders only celebrate the sale. And while that's important, it is equally important to celebrate the work that went into making the sale happen. The work ethic, better stated, your work ethic, will lead you to more sales than any other element in your sales arsenal. If someone says, "Oh that Mary, she really works hard." I consider that to be a compliment of the highest order.

You know what to do, you just don't do it. Salespeople are the smartest people in the world. As I go from audience to audience they all have one common theme among them: everyone already knows everything. Problem is they are not doing it. There's a big difference between knowing and doing, and most salespeople are without a clue about the power of the subtlety. As you read through this book don't tell yourself, "I know that." Rather ask yourself, "How good am I at that?" That question will lead you to learning.

Time management -- what's important now?
Lessons in time management are pretty much a waste of time.
You know what to do. You even know when to do it. What
you need is a lesson in procrastination. Or lessons in higher
self-image. Or a lesson in fear of rejection. Or a lesson in
preparation. Those lessons will allow you to execute the
things that in your own mind you believe you, "don't have
time for," but in reality you are just avoiding them.

Be selfish. Do it for yourself. Selfish wins.

In order for you to be the BEST you can be for others, first you must be BEST for yourself.

If you want to be the best salesperson, first you must be the
best person. If you want to be the best dad or mom, first you
must be the best person you can be for yourself. When you
achieve best for yourself, then and only then can you be your
best for others. I know it has a selfish twinge to it, but if you
think about it long enough you will come to realize that your
short comings in all of your endeavors stem from the fact
you're not being the best person you can be first.

Principle 2

PREPARE TO WIN, OR LOSE TO SOMEONE WHO IS

- Be prepared! Boy Scout motto for more than one hundred years.
- The best ways to find information about a prospect.

Red🧩Bites

- Do your homework.
- Are you a winner? Or a whiner?
- "The workday day starts the night before."
- Work while others sleep.

"OUR REGULARLY SCHEDULED PROGRAM WILL NOT BE SEEN TONIGHT
BECAUSE YOU HAVE BILLS TO PAY AND IT WOULDN'T KILL YOU
TO WORK A FEW NIGHTS A WEEK!"

Only 5% of you will do this. The rest of you are watching TV.
(Hey, raise your hand if you're making money watching TV.
Just asking.)

Be prepared!
Boy Scout motto
for more than 100 years

What do you need to know about the prospect's business to
engage? I mean if you just walk in the door and say, "tell me a
little bit about your business" how unprepared does that make
you look? Answer: TOTALLY UNPREPARED. Prepared is going
to their website and printing out several strategic pages,
reading them, and making notes so you can ask about what
you don't understand, or need elaboration on – not ask about
them from TOTAL IGNORANCE.

NOTE: Just so we understand each other, "tell me a little about
your business," is the third dumbest thing you can say to or
ask a prospect. The second is "let me tell you a little about
my business." The prospect couldn't CARE LESS about you
or your business, and probably already knows enough to not
want to hear it again. The first most dumbest? I'll tell you later
– let's talk about where to find out information about a
prospect and his or her business before your sales call.

Let me give you an incomplete list of resources … if you have
one I missed, e-mail it to salesman@gitomer.com – get your
name up in lights on Sales Caffeine and win a sales caffeine
coffee mug "Coffee is for Closers!"

PREPARE TO WIN

1. The Internet. Don't just look up their site. Enter their company name on google.com or other multiple search engines like dogpile.com and see what pops up. There may be an article or other important information. Then enter the name of the person you're meeting with. Then enter the name of the CEO. Then tell me why you're not meeting with the CEO. (Just a little jab there.) By the way, if you look up the name of the person you're meeting with and you find nothing, that also tells you something.

2. Their literature. Even though it's we-we, it has the basic "brags" covered and may talk about shifts in emphasis and market coverage. It also tells you what they think of themselves and their products.

RED WHINE ...

"What's on TV tonight?"

3. Their vendors. Usually reluctant talkers, but they can tell you what it's like to do business with them and all about how you are going to be paid. Valuable information to say the least. Vendors are a rarely used resource.

4. Their competition. Oh man, talk about dirt, here it is. Just ask casual questions about how they win business – it will tell you what it will be like to negotiate with them. By the way, the more their competition hates them, the better they usually are. Competitors hate the people who take business away from them.

5. Their customers. Customers talk. And they are the real word on delivery, organization, quality, and the subtle information that can give you an insightful competitive advantage.

6. People in your network who may know them. A quick e-mail to your inside group asking for information will always net a fact or two and may just be the bonanza you were looking for.

7. Their other employees. Occasionally the admin will help, but don't count on it. A better bet is their PR department or their marketing department.

8. The best and least used resource: Their sales department. Salespeople will tell you anything. You can get details you won't believe.

8.5 Google yourself. Want some pain? Look up your own name. Where are you? What's your Internet position? Suppose they are looking up you, what will they find? If it's nothing, that's a report card on you.

RED SELLING RESPONSE ...

"The workday
starts the
night before."

-- Scott Crawford's
grandfather

Throw away
the clicker.

And it's not just Internet preparation. It's other research like finding mutual friends, calling a few vendors, maybe a few customers. Getting VITAL information as it relates to the buying of your product or service. One more thing in preparation. Be prepared with an objective or two about what you want to accomplish in the meeting.

Proper preparation takes time, but I assure you it's impressive to the prospect. He or she knows that you have prepared, and is silently impressed. It's an advantage that very few salespeople use. They make the fatal error of getting all their own stuff ready. PowerPoint slides, samples, literature, business cards – you know, all the same things the competition is doing. Biggest mistake in sales. And almost every salesperson makes it.

RED WHINE ...

"Who wants to go drinking?"

And it's not only preparation about the sale – it's your personal preparation for sales – your personal training. How ready are you?

Get ready baby. Turn off the TV and get ready.

PREPARE TO WIN

Free Red **Bit:** Want a list of places you can gather information about the sales call? Sure you do. Go to www.gitomer.com, register if you are a first time user, and enter the word RESEARCH in the RedBit box.

Red ♥ Bites

Do your homework. Your parents nagged you for more than a decade. Either an order, "Do your homework!" or the question you hated to hear the most, "Did you do your homework yet?" You hated it. I hated it. Everyone hated it. It may have even been your introduction to lying. What they didn't tell you is that homework doesn't stop when you graduate from school. Rather, school homework is a training ground for career homework and life homework. In order to become a success at sales or at life, the first thing you have to master is homework. Getting ready, preparing, developing questions, creating ideas, and every other facet of your sales life presupposes that you have done your homework. And so, in the words of your mother, I ask you for all time, "Have you done your homework yet?"

RED SELLING RESPONSE ...

"Drink on the weekends."

Are you a winner? Or a whiner?
I'm against whining. Whiners are avoided.
Whiners are never listened to. Whiners are
never respected. And in general nobody likes
or wants to hang around with a whiner (the
exception being other whiners–misery loves
company). In my first book, *The Sales Bible*,
I put a quote in there that said, "You can't be
a winner if you're a whiner, wiener." At the
time, I thought it was pretty funny, but over
the years, I've found that it's not only funny,
it's 100% accurate. Think for a moment about
how you bring problems to others. Think
for a moment about what you say when
something doesn't go your way. Think for
a moment about how you react when you
lose a big sale. If any of those reactions or
responses contain whining, cut it out or you'll
become a wiener, whiner.

RED WHINE ...

"I can just
wing it."

**"The workday day starts
the night before."** My friend,
Scott Crawford, and I had
breakfast together one morning
at Einstein's. We started to talk
philosophically about sales and
business, and out of the blue,
he dropped this gem: "My
grandfather always told me,
'Scott, the workday starts the
night before.'" I ran to get a

napkin so I could write it down. I asked Scott to tell me more and he did. It was all about preparing. It was all about getting ready for the next day. I can inflict major pain on you right now by asking what it is that you do to get ready for your next sales day. Your answer is somewhere between drinking, watching sporting events, or watching TV reruns. How pathetic is that? Well, actually some people don't consider that pathetic. They would be your competition.

Work while others sleep. I wake up early every day. I run to my computer and I begin to write. I've been doing that for 12 years. So far the net is five books, 700 columns, not to mention 1,000 presentations to companies all over the world. Before you get up in the morning, I'm already making money. I usually stay up until about 1:00 a.m. From 11:00 p.m. 'til 1:00 a.m., things are quiet. Like anybody, sometimes I fiddle on the Internet. Yes I'm an Ebay addict, but I also surf around to clients' websites just to see what's going on. To see if I can learn anything new. And to see if I can come up with any ideas. I've only been doing that for five years. The point is I take those extra three or four hours a day and earn more in that time, when most people are asleep, than they do when they're awake.

RED SELLING RESPONSE ...

"Wing it and lose to someone who doesn't."

Principle 3

PERSONAL BRANDING IS SALES: IT'S NOT WHO YOU KNOW, IT'S WHO KNOWS YOU

- **Brand Me.**

Red🅡Bites

- Build your personal brand and customers will call you.
  Build your personal brand and customers will be loyal.

- Position more, compete less.

- Who sees you? Who appoints you? It depends on who knows you!

- Who values you and your knowledge?

"THE FIRST ISSUE OF MY CUSTOMER E-ZINE WAS EXCELLENT!
FOR MY SECOND ISSUE, I'M HAVING TROUBLE FINDING
SOMETHING NEW TO SAY."

Brand "Me" –
Execution for results …

Personal Branding is not complicated, unless you take a course in it. Then it's scary as hell. Entrepreneurial Personal Branding and marketing is much easier.

I have a brand. Or should I say: *I AM the brand*. I have taken my name, "Gitomer" and "Jeffrey Gitomer" and turned it into my brand. My column has been in the *Charlotte Business Journal* every week for twelve years. It's now in 90 markets. My website is my name: gitomer.com. My company is my name: BuyGitomer. And everything I do has my name on it. (I even registered the URLs for the misspellings of my name.)

What's your brand? Not just your company brand – I'm talking about your *personal* brand. In sales, prospects buy the salesperson FIRST. If they buy brand-you, then they may buy what you're selling. How do you get a brand? How do you create a brand?

First: If you're a small business person, don't read a book on it. I have yet to find one that is pragmatic enough to work. Second, think "me" and "give-to-get." Third, think "promotion combined with advertising." And the kicker – it's how hard you work, how smart you work, and how dedicated you are, combined with your self-belief, that will help your brand proliferate more than anything.

Personal branding is ...

• **Create demand for your product or service indirectly.** (Through means other than direct advertising.)

• **Get the business community to have confidence in you** – as a respected high caliber individual.

• **Get the business community to have confidence in your business** – Earn a reputation for quality performance so good that it's talked about.

• **Establish yourself as an expert** – Why just be in the field, when you can be perceived on top of it?

• **Be seen and known as a leader** – Stand in front of the group, and tell them or get involved in a group and lead them. Show up where everyone is – all the time.

• **Be known as an innovator.** Be known as a person or business of value. Be known as a resource.

• **Separate yourself from competition** – Get in front of the pack and set a standard.

• **Gain professional stature** – Your image is determined by others. Your outreach determines your image.

• **Build your image** – and the image of your business – by being a consistent positive performer. By associating with quality things and people. By delivering what you promise. Get talked about in a positive way.

• **As a result of your total branding and marketing outreach** – make your phone ring with qualified prospects – then convert them to sales.

"HEY JEFFREY, GET SPECIFIC!" you scream. OK, OK. Here's some branding information you won't find in any textbook. It's the actions I have taken over the past 15 years to build my brand.

I cannot guarantee that they will work for you. But they do work. I can tell you that first-hand. *Here's my personal formula for developing a personal brand:*

• **Register your name.com** … go to www.obtainyourname.com or some name registration site, and register your name as fast as you can. Register your kids' names, too.

• **Be willing to give of yourself-- first** … It's not the only way, but it is the best and most long-lasting one I've found.

PERSONAL BRANDING

RED SELLING RESPONSE …

"If you brand yourself people will know you."

• **Dedicate time to make it happen** … Or it won't happen. If you want to make a lasting mark, it must be preceded with a master plan.

• **Get others to help you** … List the people you think can help or help you connect – and ask for their support. (The easiest way to get support? Give it first – without keeping score.)

• **Make a brief 30-second commercial** … About what you do and how you can help others. Deliver it AFTER you have asked the other person what they do.

• **Combine outreaches** … Example:
  – Get your charity to get you into the community as a spokesperson.
  – Donate a scholarship to the trade association of your best client.
  – Give a talk and donate the speaking fee to your charity.
  – Make a donation in honor of a significant event in a customer's life.

RED WHINE ...

"My company isn't supporting my sales effort."

• **Do everything with a creative flair** … Something that makes the time and effort you gave worth remembering. Memorability is a vital link to building market awareness.

• **Get the best business card money can buy** … It's your image – and it makes an impact every time you give one – either wow, positive, mediocre or negative. Engrave it, blind emboss it, foil stamp it, logo it, graphic design it, multi-color it. Here's the acid test: When you give out your card, if someone doesn't look at it and say, "Nice card," get it redone.

• **Stay in front of the people you want to do business with** … By combining your outreaches, you can create a steady flow of your images (in the paper, weekly e-zine, on TV, your newsletter, etc.) to your target market. It takes between five and ten images to create awareness great enough to make a buying decision.

• **Become a resource** … It's much more powerful than someone perceiving you as a salesman or entrepreneur. People will want to be around you, and pay attention to what you say, if they believe what you say and do has value to them and their business.

• **Persistence and consistency are the secrets** … Don't do anything once – and then sit back and wait. You must keep plugging without expectation. If you're good, have patience. Your phone will ring.

PERSONAL BRANDING

RED SELLING RESPONSE …

"Find another company."

• **Have a good time doing it.** People who take it too serious have problems sorting out what's important in the world. Treat it like an important game. Play as hard as you can to win.

• **Strive to be the best at whatever you do.** Go for the personal goal – be the best. Not the material goal – make a lot of money. Be the best and the money will automatically show up.

• **Ignore idiots and zealots.** There are a lot of jealous people and nay-sayers in the world. Ignore them. People who rain on your parade – because they have no parade of their own.

RED WHINE ...

"They are making me cold call."

Become known as a person of action ...

The result of these actions will be a person who is known for getting things done – a leader. It's not just a reflection on you – it's a reflection on your company, the products and services you offer, and your personal brand. It's something you can't place a value on or buy, but it's the difference between sale and no sale. And the difference between having to sell, and people wanting to buy. The result of these actions will be a brand new you.

Free Red✗Bit: Want a few more steps to branding success? Go to www.gitomer.com, register if you are a first time user, and enter BRAND ME in the RedBit box.

Red♠Bites

Build your personal brand and customers will call you. Build your personal brand and customers will be loyal. The law of attraction is created by your brand. Let me use myself as an example. My brand gets me in your door. I write a column, "Sales Moves" every week that appears in 90 papers. I have a weekly e-mail magazine, "Sales Caffeine," that delivers valuable sales information to more than 100,000 people each week. From those two extensions of my brand I receive not less than 10,000 web hits or inquiries each week. And if you look at the way I've established the brand over the years you'll see that I fight for the brand's integrity. I didn't say I'm pristine. I didn't say I'm politically correct. I didn't say I'm not on the edge (sometimes over the edge).

PERSONAL BRANDING

RED SELLING RESPONSE ...

"If you brand yourself, prospects will call YOU."

That's my persona. The integrity of my brand is the consistency and the value of the message. I have become known as "THE sales guy." All because I brand myself with information that others can use to make more sales and build their business. It's important to note that in the 12 years I've been writing my column, I have never made a sales call to book a seminar. They call me first because they know me and I have provided them with value. Every branding book talks about getting the customer to remember your name at the time they are ready to purchase. And while that's a correct statement, it speaks nothing of the critical aspect, "Will they buy from you?" And, "will they buy from you," is all about their perception of the value of your brand. That is what creates the law of attraction.

Position more, compete less. My article appears in more than 90 cities around the country. Am I the best salesperson in cities like Dallas, St. Louis, or Atlanta? Doesn't matter. I'm the best positioned salesperson in those cities. My picture is in the paper. My competition reads my column every week and hates my guts. I'm better positioned in their city than they are. They live there, I don't. My position gives me a competitive selling edge, people already know me. The rule of sales that applies in this situation, "In sales, it's not who you know. In sales, it's who knows you." Positioning helps you get known.

Who sees you? Who appoints you? It depends on who knows you! One other aspect of positioning is how high up the ladder you can get when you actually make an appointment. Because of the status I have, or better stated the market positioning I have, I'm always able to meet with a company's leader. Sometimes it's the CEO, sometimes it's the owner. But it's always the person who "runs the place." This gives me an incredible competitive advantage. In that number one, they already know me so I don't have to build credibility when I walk in the door. And number two, they are always the decision maker. If you're meeting with a CEO that already knows and respects you, I can promise you one thing, a lot of yeses will come your way.

Who values you and your knowledge?
Most salespeople stop at the end of the selling process. They go through the same old crapola of prospect, appoint, present, close, follow-up. That sales strategy will lead you no place but to another sales job. If you want to build a relationship, if you want to get referrals, you have to become known as an expert or the expert in whatever you do. This requires hard work and study on your part. If you're not willing to do that, my immediate recommendation is run down to the post office and get a nice safe job down there selling stamps at the counter. If your customers value the knowledge and the expertise that you have delivered to them, they will think long and hard before they entertain the dregs of humanity who also sell your product. You may know them as your competitors.

In sales, it's not who you know.
In sales, it's who knows you.

PERSONAL BRANDING

Principle 4

IT'S ALL ABOUT VALUE, IT'S ALL ABOUT RELATIONSHIP, IT'S NOT ALL ABOUT PRICE

- **The 6.5 principles of giving value and being valuable.**
- **Free Speech.**
- **Price vs. Value, the REAL way to beat "price."**

RedBites

- Give value first, don't add it.
- Make friends before you start, or don't start.
- Act professionally, talk friendly.
- Sales for the moment. Friends for life.
  Sales for the commission. Value for the fortune.

"IF YOU'RE NOT ABSOLUTELY THRILLED AND DELIGHTED WITH OUR PRODUCT, CALL US TOLL-FREE AND WE'LL BE HAPPY TO HELP YOU ESTABLISH MORE REASONABLE EXPECTATIONS."

Where is "value" in the sales equation?

What role does "value" play in making sales?

What role does "value" play
in building customer loyalty?

How does "value" help build
solid business relationships?

The word "value" has a difficult time being defined
and understood.

Giving value and adding value are words that many
salespeople and sales executives have a difficult time in
understanding, let alone providing. Most people think that
value is all about something the company adds. Some small
additional service, something tacked onto the product, a slight
reduction in price, even something "free." Wrong.

These things are promotions, not values. Value is something
done for the customer, in favor of the customer.

In my case, I have found that it is most effective to give value
first. And give it without expectation, and give it often, and
give it without expectation and give it to your best prospects.
And did I mention give it without expectation?

I give value through my weekly column and weekly e-zine.
People call me out of the blue and thank me, ask for my
information, and hire me.

The mantra is simple: I put myself in front of people who can
say "yes" to me and I deliver value first. Make it your mantra.

GIVING VALUE

The 6.5 principles of giving value and being valuable ...

1. **Market with stuff and information about prospects and customers -- not about you.** They will NEVER read your brochure – in fact they'll probably throw it away. Send them information about how they profit, produce or succeed, and they will devour EVERY WORD.

2. **Write (good) stuff in journals, newspapers, e-zines, and newsletters.** Writing creates a perceived leadership position (your picture is in print), and is a value positioning statement at the same time. It also allows those who agree with your ideas or philosophy to connect with you.

RED WHINE ...
"They keep throwing away my brochure."

3. **Create response vehicles or mechanisms in everything you write.** If they agree with you and want more, offer it. It's a great way to connect with business. Lack of response is also a report card.

4. Earn your way onto every broadcast media possible. Try to get on a talk show with information everyone can use. Tie your expertise to a timely topic or holiday. (NOTE: Everyone can get on a talk show tomorrow with these two words – call in.)

5. Get known as a person of value. Get known to get business to come to you. Leading a group or committee at the Chamber of Commerce, charity volunteerism. (HINT: Pick one you really like).

6. Send your stuff after they ask for it, and make sure it has something they will keep. Proactive mailings rarely work. If you really want to test the viability of your information, offer it and see who wants it. I send nothing until someone calls and asks for it. (NOTE: What is the value of your brochure? If it's stated in terms of you, you could put the words "up-yours," anywhere in the middle of it, and no one would ever find it.)

6.5 Speak in public or cold call? I say speak. Why? How? Turn the page …

RED SELLING RESPONSE …

"They don't want your brochure. They want answers to their situations and concerns."

GIVING VALUE

To speak or not to speak …

Free Speech. The legacy you leave to yourself.

Want 50 new leads a week?
Give a free speech at a civic group.

Many salespeople looking to emerge are frantically trying to "market" themselves from brochures to direct mail to cold calling to networking. Expensive frustration. The best way to market yourself is give yourself to the market. Expose yourself to your prospects.

My advice: Free speech. Or to put it a clearer way – speak for free. Free speech pays. Big pay. And free speech has rewards. Big rewards.

NOTE WELL: I said "speech" not "sales pitch."

When you show up at a civic organization to deliver a free 15-20 minute talk, here's the gold you receive:

• **You get to give a live sales presentation to sell YOURSELF, not your product or service.**

 • **You get to do an audition -- right in front of the decision maker.**

• **You build (and strengthen) your network.**

• **You (re)establish your presence.**

• **You help the community.**

• **You build your speaking skills, your presentation skills, and storytelling skills.**

• **You get to try out new material.**

• **You will attract new customers (all leaders).**

• **If you're just starting out in your business -- you will have a great opportunity to move up the ladder.**

• **You get a chance to have meaningful impact on someone through your words.**

• **You eat for free.**

Now, to some of the above "rewards" you may want to add the prefix phrase, "if you're great," to get the real meaning and make the most impact, but I think the message is clear.

Interested? Just contact any civic organization in your city. They are dying for a good talk. Every week they go looking for GOOD speakers. And it sure beats cold calling.

Want the best strategy of approach?
Here are 6.5 SUCCESS TACTICS of Free Speech:

1. Don't give a sales pitch, but do speak on your topic.
Speak about interesting stuff to the audience that teases your stuff – BUT give a great speech. If you sell burglar alarms speak about home safety, if you sell copiers, speak about image and productivity. Get it?

2. Pick a great audience. There are groups and there are groups – pick the best ones. Highest profile, most likely to have the bigwigs.

GIVING VALUE

3. Give a handout. Even just a few pages, a handout will help the audience follow along – and it precludes you from having to memorize the talk – and gives every member of the audience a way to contact you. WARNING: Give out the handout when you start to use it – NEVER BEFORE YOU BEGIN. If you give out the handout before you start your talk, people will read one thing while you're speaking about another, and (worse) you lose audience control and the impact of your message.

4. Videotape it. After the talk you can play the video at home and see how good you REALLY are as opposed to how good you THINK you are.

5. Ask for audience evaluations. Read about your impact, if any.

6. Give value, get leads. At the end of your talk, offer something additional for free in exchange for their card. The cards you get are LEADS.

6.5 Hang around after the meeting. That's when you find out what your impact was and who your best prospects are.

DON'T SELL YOUR STUFF AT THE MEETING. Make a lunch appointment or breakfast meeting, and avoid making a sales pitch or bragging about your company.

On a personal note, this is how I got started getting paid to speak. From my weekly column in the paper, several Rotary and Kiwanis clubs in town called me to give a talk. I decided NOT to talk on sales (my expertise), rather I spoke about children (my favorite topic) and titled a talk, "What we've learned from our kids."

I selected seven skills my kids had helped me strengthen in the rearing process (like imagination, persistence, blind faith, enthusiasm), and told a brief story about each. In 20 minutes I made the audience laugh, cry, think, and learn.

I had a handout, and also offered the seven best parenting rules I'd ever learned (for free) if they would just give me their card. At the end of every meeting, I ALWAYS had at least 50 cards, and one PAID talk from someone who said, "How'd you like to come speak to my employees?"

So my rewards (and yours) for giving a free 20-minute talk included a live audition and sales call in front of 100 decision makers, audience impact, new friends, a self-taught lesson, a practice session, a free lunch, a pen (their usual gift for the talk), a certificate of thanks from the group, 50 warm leads, and a paid engagement. Beats direct mail, or cold calling.

BONUS TIP: Any group will pay you $100 if you have them make the check out to your favorite charity in your name and theirs.

No matter who you are or where you are in your sales career, free speech can impact learning and earning. Free speech isn't just a right – it's an opportunity. Exercise yours.

Free Red⋀Bit: Want a few presentation tips? Tips on how to give a better speech, and a better sales presentation. Go to www.gitomer.com, register if you are a first time user, and enter the word PRESENTATION in the RedBit box.

Price vs. Value,
The REAL way to beat "price"
How much is it?
Answer: Doesn't matter
if the value is there.

Let me make it real simple – draw a line down the middle of a flipchart page. On one side put up "price too high" and "take the lowest bid" – on the other side of the page I want you to tell me what your customer wants – no not your product – what your customer REALLY wants – it may have nothing to do with your product or service.

What do your customers want? Your customer wants:

- **More sales**
- **Greater productivity**
- **More profit**
- **Better image**
- **More customers**
- **Loyal employees**
- **Better morale**
- **No hassles**
- **More free time**
- **Notoriety**

If you are able to get him or her those or even one of those items, how significant is price? The more value you provide, the less price matters.

The classic example of price vs. perceived value is in the automobile business. You've all seen an ad from car dealers that sell "a dollar over invoice," "at invoice," or, "below invoice." No value. Certainly no perceived value. What happens after I take ownership? How will I value from the "use" of my purchase? What kind of service can I expect?

If one of them would place a full page ad in the paper that said, "Our prices are guaranteed to be $100 more than anybody else's price, but our service is guaranteed to be 100% better than anybody else's service." And underneath that are pictures of five customers telling you in one form or another why they paid the extra $100 and that the service is phenomenal. They would have all the business.

I promise you that no one remembers the price at 7:00 a.m. when you are waiting in line at a car dealership for service, and you don't get taken until 7:30, and the service person is somewhat rude, and they have no loaner cars so someone else has to drive there with you and take you to work, and when you get back at 5:00 p.m. to pick your car up you wait another 20 minutes and come to find out they didn't have the part for what was broken, and you have to come back again next week. But you were the smartest guy in the world. You saved $100 on the car. At that moment you would have paid an extra $1,000 for the car.

GIVING VALUE

Here's the lost opportunity:
The salesperson concentrating on "making the best deal" and going through every sales hoodwinking gyration, neglected to talk about what it would be like to have the car serviced. When there's no value all that's left is price. Now I used the car dealer example because every one of you has had it happen to you in one form or another.

What you need to do now is figure out where your value proposition lies AND how to communicate it in a way that the customer will get it AND be so compelling in your proof statements or your testimonials that the customer will both emotionally and logically make the decision to buy from you.

Understand this ... The sale is emotionally driven and emotionally decided. Then it is justified logically. The head is attached to the price. The heart is attached to the wallet.
Here's what you need to start:

1. Stop thinking of your product as a commodity.
If you tell yourself you're selling a commodity, you are doomed to selling price. Wireless phone, commodity. Not. Office supplies, commodity. Not. Computer hardware, commodity. Not.

RED WHINE ...

"The guy said he only had 5 minutes and wanted my price."

It's all about the relationship. It's all about the perceived value. Let's get one thing straight before we go any further. Not everyone will buy value. Thirty to forty percent of all customers will buy price. That's the bad news. The good news is 60-70% of all customers will buy value if you provide it to them. Lowest price is lowest profit. Every time you take a nickel off the top line price, you are subtracting that same nickel off the bottom line profit of the same sale. And here's the reality about people who buy price only: Cheap bastards are also a pain in the ass.

2. Take the last 10 sales that you made and try to discover the following: How was the sale completed? In other words what went into the decision making process? Who pulled the trigger? In other words, the lower down the scale you are the more price matters. If you're a hotel and you're trying to sell a meeting to a corporation, the meeting planner is going to be much more price oriented and comparison oriented than the CEO who has the responsibility for the outcome of the meeting. Twenty dollars a night/room may be an obstacle at the meeting planner level, but it's nothing to a CEO who wants his people to be happy, well rested, and productive for the real purpose of the meeting. Which brings me to my next point.

RED SELLING RESPONSE ...

"They don't want your sales pitch. They want answers to their situations and concerns."

GIVING VALUE

3. Don't focus on the sale, focus on the lifetime use of the product or the service. Get your probable purchaser to visualize what life will be like after they take ownership. If you can concentrate on use and ownership, then you can focus on cost and long term value as opposed to price. The key is that the customer must visualize this at a time when they are also focusing on "how much is it?"

Let me make one more side note here. Sometimes the price is precluded by someone who says to you, "We've spent our whole budget." That person is not a decision maker. He or she is a budget spender. And the entire time they are spending their budget they are predominantly focused on price. My goal when I'm in a sales situation is to somehow get to the person that makes the budget. The person that makes the budget can add a zero and make another budget.

RED WHINE ...

"Another three bid, take the lowest price, no profit proposal."

Back to the process. What I'm basically saying is …

4. Start your sales call at a higher level. The higher up the corporate ladder you can get, the less price matters. The higher the officer in the company, the more they are able to see the big picture of profit and productivity as opposed to price. Here's the acid test to see if you're talking to the right person: When someone starts to hammer you for price, you simply say, "Price or profit Mr. Jones. Which would you rather have? Price lasts for a moment Mr. Jones, profit lasts for a life-time." All executive corporate officers are interested in making more profit.

Here's the problem. What I've just challenged you to do will double your workload as a salesperson. You now have to go into the sale with productivity ideas and profit ideas. The good news is not only will your workload double, your sales will double along with it. The better news is most salespeople will not do the hard work that it takes to make selling easy. There's not much competition at the top of the sales ladder. But the best news is you will be in control of your own outcomes.

"But Jeffrey, you don't understand. All of my sales are on three bids and the customer takes the lowest bid." No, Sparky. You don't understand. You're not using any imagination to try and change the terms of the proposal. Why don't you recommend to your customer, "Mr. Jones, all three of the prices you are going to receive are going to be within 10% of one another. Why don't we state in the contract that if all prices are within 10% that you are free to choose the product or

RED SELLING RESPONSE ...
"If you offer no value, all that's left is your price."

GIVING VALUE

the service that you believe will help your company the most. Or, the company you have the most confidence in performing after the sale. Fair enough?"

Or why don't you say, "Mr. Jones, all of us salespeople are going to make claims about how great we are. I recommend you add to each proposal that each of us potential vendors supply you with video testimonial from other customers proving that what we say is true."

I've just given you two ideas on how to change lowest price proposals. But you can use these same ideas if no bidding is involved. Let's take a moment and look at your scurrilous rat competition that comes in at the last second and tries to lower price to steal business. First understand that if you know it's coming or has the potential of coming you can discuss this with your potential customer. You can ward this off from occurring by agreeing with the customer that it will not occur. And also agreeing on why. Most of that will occur after the delivery of the product or service has taken place. People who buy price have no vision. They are not looking beyond the moment of purchase. Your job is to make certain that the customer has a clear view of how they will profit after the sale has taken place. And that the profit is greater than their desire to buy lower price.

The sales and marketing philosophy of Jeffrey Gitomer:

I put myself in front of people who can say yes to me, and I deliver value first.

Red Bites

Give value first, don't add it. I have never understood the philosophy of "value added," and I'm willing to make a bet you don't even know the definition of it. Typically, it's a bunch of baloney from your company for a few minor services or other trifles that your competitor could easily duplicate. It does nothing to set you apart or increase the probability of a sale. My sales philosophy is different. It's called "value first." Simply put, I put value in the hands of my potential customers before I ever ask them to buy anything. If you read my column in the paper, if you get my weekly sales e-zine called *Sales Caffeine*, if you visit my website, you'll find tons of ideas and valuable sales information that I give away each week for free. I've been doing that for twelve years. It has earned me millions of dollars. First I give it away THEN I reap the rewards. I don't have much of a brochure, I do almost no advertising and I make no sales calls. Pretty ass backwards for a sales organization, wouldn't you say? It defies every rule or law of marketing you'll ever find in a textbook, except for one minor little item: It works. Find something that your customer considers valuable and give it away. It only needs to be information that will help him or her build their business so you can earn yours. Word of caution: My method of selling or should I say, getting the customer to buy, takes hard work and most salespeople are not willing to do the hard work that it takes to make selling easy.

Make friends before you start, or don't start.
When I meet a prospect on a sales call, the first thing I do is establish some kind of rapport that includes finding some common ground. I laugh with them, I talk to them about them. I establish some credibility with them and then I begin my sales presentation. I would rather walk out of a sales presentation from a prospect who says, "Let's get right down to business." What he's really saying is, let's get right down to "How much is it?" I don't win sales on price. I win sales on friendship. I give the "price sales" to someone else. They're the biggest pain in the ass on the planet, and so are the people associated with them.

Act professionally, talk friendly. Too many salespeople think they have to be professional in order to gain buyer credibility. Nothing could be further from the truth. Me? I'm friendly. I try to act as professionally as I can but I always err on the side of being too friendly. The stiff sales professional will give a bid or proposal and if it ain't the lowest, he walks away with a goose egg. Me? I'm the friendliest and I'm the highest. I wonder if there is a correlation there? Now I'm not saying be the highest price (although it seems to be working for companies like BMW and Mercedes Benz), but I am saying be the friendliest.

Sales for the moment. Friends for life. Sales for the commission. Value for the fortune. Early on in my writing career I created a quote, "If you make a sale, you can earn a commission. If you make a friend, you can earn a fortune." This philosophy is rarely used in sales. Those who employ it are the top performers and the top paid salespeople. They build relationships. They don't worry about their quotas. They concentrate on the value they provide to their customers and the corresponding orders that accompany it. I challenge you that this is the single hardest lesson to learn and at the same time, it is the single most powerful and most financially rewarding lesson that I teach. It is the essence of my philosophy, it is the core of my business, and it is the heart of my success. Make it yours and earn a fortune.

All things being equal, people want to do business with their friends.

All things being not quite so equal, people STILL want to do business with their friends.

GIVING VALUE

Principle 5

IT'S NOT WORK, IT'S NETWORK

- **The 21.5 best places to network.**

Red R Bites
- Get face to face first.
- Networking eliminates cold calling.
- Networking leads to referrals.

"I SPEND 99 PERCENT OF MY TIME NETWORKING LOCALLY, BUILDING A STRONG WEB PRESENCE, ESTABLISHING BENEFICIAL RELATIONSHIPS WITH LEADERS IN MY FIELD, SPEAKING TO BUSINESS AND CIVIC GROUPS, AND PARTICIPATING IN CHARITABLE COMMUNITY OUTREACH ACTIVITIES. I SPEND THE OTHER ONE PERCENT TRYING TO REMEMBER WHAT IT IS I ACTUALLY DO FOR A LIVING!"

The 21.5 best places to network
(and the secrets to being successful at it)

How important is networking?
Real important.

What can networking do for your relationships?
Build them.

What can networking do for your sales?
Make them.

What can networking do for your success?
*The right contacts and connections
can make or break it.*

If you're trying to be successful, it's the difference between mediocre and big.

If networking is so important, why aren't you out there doing more of it?

Here are the big four reasons:

1. You think it takes too much time, and you are unwilling to dedicate time.

2. You have a "they don't pay me enough money to do this" attitude, and you are doomed to negativity and mediocrity.

3. You think cold calling is a great way to prospect.

4. You want to, but you don't know how or where.

If you're #4, I can help you. And this information is vital to making a successful networking plan. If you're #1-3, this information is not for you, but don't worry, you already know everything anyway, so this would just be a review.

Networking is life skills and social skills combined with sales skills.

It's business leisure conducted before and after work – as opposed to business frantic, which is conducted from 9 to 5 (the exception being lunch).

RED WHINE ...

"I'm gonna blow off that boring association dinner."

Networking is a mandatory function of business for salespeople and entrepreneurs. But everyone in every segment of commerce and career networks. Great scientists, electrical engineers, and surgeons all have their annual meeting of some kind where they get together and "talk shop." Giant trade shows attract buyers and sellers from all over the world.

What are the principles of networking?

- to get known by those who count
- to get more prospects
- to make more contacts
- to make more sales
- to build relationships
- to make a career advancement (or just get a job)
- to build your reputation (and be seen and known as consistent)

What do you need to be a successful networker?

- **A GREAT 30-second commercial** that engages and asks questions that qualify the prospect, and gets to the next step in the sales cycle if there's an interest.

- **Your willingness** to dedicate the time it takes to do it and be excellent at it.

- **A plan** of where and when.

RED SELLING RESPONSE ...

"Networking is becoming known by those who count, and you can only become known by showing up (prepared)."

It's Not Work

To maximize your networking effectiveness, you must follow one simple rule:

RULE A1A -- go where your customers and prospects go, or are likely to be.

Ok, here we go -- the 21.5 BEST places to network are:

1. Chamber of Commerce business event after hours. Tried and true. They always net a few contacts and renew old friendships. They are also a GREAT place to try out your new 30-second personal commercial. NOTE: Often at a business networking event everyone's trying to sell – you gotta be able to wear either the buyer or seller hat, and listen for your opportunity.

2. A high level Chamber of Commerce event. Board of directors or advisors meeting. Annual dinner. The Chamber of Commerce is your best local networking resource, IF you take advantage of it.

3. Any *Business Journal* event. Forty under forty, power breakfasts, seminars. Places where movers and shakers go. The *Business Journal* reader and event attendee demographics are staggering. They are ALL people who make things happen.

4. A networking club or business organization where solid business contacts belong and participate. In Charlotte it's groups like the Metrolina Entrepreneurial Council, the Hood Hargett Breakfast Club, and the Metrolina Business Council. The more you attend, the more you get known, grow, and succeed in your market.

5. Someplace where like-minded people belong. The Touchdown Club, your college alumni club, the ACT users club. Having common ground always gets a conversation going.

6. Any type of class you take to learn more and make yourself better. Toastmaster's, Dale Carnegie, even learning a foreign language. Other people who want to improve will also be there. You will improve and make lifetime friendships.

7. A civic organization. Rotary, Kiwanis, Elks, Moose, Lions. Any civic animal will do. Meetings are a great place to build relationships with others, and help the community at the same time. SUCCESS HINT: Be a leader not just a member.

8. Attend a cultural event. The theater and the symphony attract people with class and money. Take in a show and meet them.

9. Get involved with a charity or be a community volunteer – Everything from the American Cancer Society to the symphony society have people who help behind the scenes. Be one of them.

10. Your trade or professional association. This is the best place to learn about your product, your competition AND your customers at the same time.

11. Your best customer(s) trade or professional association. This is the great place to learn more about your customers AND get introduced to your prospects. SUCCESS HINT: Be a seminar presenter, not just an attendee.

12. Trade shows. Both industry specific and general business shows are excellent places to get known, get sales, and get ahead. Take the success hint from above and add the ingredient of hard work, rather than partying, and you have the formula for trade show success. It may be your best networking venue of them all, and most people waste it on having a "non-stop-whoop-it-up-we're-away-from-home" attitude.

13. Join a private club. A golf country club, a food and networking club like Club Corp. with branches all over the US, or a small private club. In Charlotte, it's Belle Acres, America's premier private club. Great food (Mike the chef is beyond superb). Great atmosphere (fascinating memorabilia on every wall). Great service (always with a smile and some humor). Great owner (Bud Mingles and his dry wit adds to the fun of being there). Oh, and great networking (every Charlotte big-wig eventually eats at Belle Acres).

14. Meal networking. Invite a prospect to dine. Then invite a prospect for him or her. While in the restaurant, see who else is in the bar. Hop around without being rude. Introduce everyone you meet to whoever you brought. Make it ultra friendly. Compliment everyone in your introduction. PERSONAL NOTE: I have my morning breakfast at Einstein's Bagels. I love the food and service. I have all my morning meetings there. I ALWAYS meet other people there. My breakfast meeting is always to do a deal. And often my chance meetings result in business. SUCCESS HINT: Own a restaurant or three. Places where you frequent and know the owners and managers. It plays a major role in your meal networking.

15. Health club. Exercise and network. Get healthy and wealthy at the same time. In Charlotte, it's the "Y." Join the "in" club, and get "in" shape to win.

16. Sports events. Both games and tailgates. Everyone eventually goes to the ball game. And for the competitive sports nut within you, play The Networking Game. It's in my book *The Sales Bible*.

17. Parents of your children's friends. If you have a big prospect whose kid plays ball in the same league as your kid, you'll have a big advantage to make him a big customer.

18. Happy hour. Can be a great place to make a quick connection. Just don't get too happy.

19. Karaoke. Not only do you have a blast and meet people, you also improve your presentation skills every time you sing a song.

20. Neighborhood homeowner's association/condo association. Get to know your neighbors and who they know.

21. The airplane. I don't mean you need to meet every passenger, but get to know your seatmate. You never know who they know until you ask. I always try to sell a book to the person sitting next to me. It's fun, it's practice, and it's profitable.

21.5 Being ready to network when you get there. Woody Allen says 90% of success is showing up. And he's almost right. Ninety percent of success is showing up PREPARED. Having your personal commercial, or cocktail commercial, or one minute hook ready to spin at a moment's notice is evidence of your networking prowess – or not.

OK, I've given you the meat.

Here's your personal action plan:
List the possible areas -- every one of them.

Figure out who goes there now and who MAY be there.
Figure out what business enticement you have and start there.

Secret: Get respected by those who count – don't just attend – get involved and lead.

Big secret: The key advantage is that networking is relaxed: business leisure. The workday is busy: business frantic. You'll get more done and see more people in the leisure zone.

Biggest secret: Be aware of who is around you wherever they are. The danger of that is not paying attention to the person you are talking to. Another word for that would be: RUDE. But the moment you're free, your peripheral vision must be 360 degrees. The more you pay attention, the more it will pay.

It is important to note that these "best places to network" are not just ideas and suggestions. Every item listed above is something I do personally, and have had MAJOR success with. These are things I do, not just things I teach.

Make contacts, make sales, eliminate cold calling, build your career, build relationships, build your reputation, and make friends. I have met my life-long best friends networking – and I also do business with them – thousands of dollars worth.

How many life-long friends do you make cold calling?

Free Red✕Bit: Want Harvey Mackay's ten rules of networking? We have been given permission to excerpt a page from THE BEST NETWORKING BOOK EVER: Harvey Mackay's *Dig Your Well Before You're Thirsty*. Go to www.gitomer.com, register if you are a first time user, and enter the words DIG YOUR WELL in the RedBit box.

I HAVE A
CHALLENGE FOR YOU:
Between now
and next week,
attend three
networking functions
from the list above.

I guarantee you will make more contacts, build more relationships, and maybe even make a sale or two.

To make the most of a networking event, spend 75% of your time with people you don't know.

– Jeffrey Gitomer

Red  Bites

Get face to face first. Meeting someone on the phone (cold calling them – even from a referral) is not the best way to start any relationship. It can work, I'm just saying it's not the best way. When you meet someone face to face you can see them and hear them at the same time. This is 100 times more insightful. Networking is the best way to create initial face to face meetings. It doesn't just have to be a business after hours type of thing. It can also be a three way lunch, a trade association meeting, even an annual convention. The reason face to face is so powerful is that your prospect can get to like you faster. The more they like you the more they will buy from you. Networking builds rapport that leads to appointments and sales. Lots of sales.

Networking eliminates cold calling. As I've stated 1,000 times before, I consider cold calling a waste of time. Either by phone or knocking on doors you're interrupting someone by trying to barge in and sell something. It works, but not very often. And cold calling (or should I say lack of ability to cold call) is the single biggest cause of job turnover. Consider for a moment your annual convention or trade show. One hundred exhibitors, maybe more, with decision makers milling about. People you couldn't get to see within a year of cold calling are all in the same room at the same time. What could you be thinking? If you meet them first and they like you, you will have an easier time getting your phone call through and making a meeting. And think of it in the reverse. Suppose you cold call someone and then saw them at a tradeshow. What would you say to that guy?

"Hey remember me? I'm the guy that cold called you and you hung up."

Networking leads to referrals. Not every networking contact is a direct prospect for your business. Through an advanced networking technique called netweaving created by Bob Littel in Atlanta, GA (www.netweaving.com), you can help other people find resources at a networking event. When you do this, you will find that other people will help you. In addition, you can go to a networking event where your customers go and they may just introduce you to other people like themselves, who may also be willing to buy from you.

Networking works well when you employ the two-word secret: Show up.

Networking works best when you employ the three-word secret: Show up prepared.

Principle 6

IF YOU CAN'T GET IN FRONT OF THE REAL DECISION MAKER, YOU SUCK

- The reasons you can't get appointments.
- Will the real decision maker please stand up.

RedBites

- Can't get past the gatekeeper? You suck!
- Can't get your voicemail returned? You suck!

"I'M NOT LAUGHING AT YOUR JOKES. I'M LAUGHING AT THE IDEA THAT YOU THINK I HAVE ENOUGH AUTHORITY TO MAKE A DECISION AROUND HERE!"

The reasons you can't get appointments.

The guy won't appoint me.

I can't get through to the decision maker.

He won't commit to an appointment.

She won't return my phone call.

He has rescheduled me three times in two weeks.

He didn't show for his appointment.

Quit your whining. Those aren't real reasons. Those are symptoms or wake-up calls to the fact that your fundamental sales skills are lacking.

Why are you not setting appointments?

Easy answer: No compelling reason on the part of the buyer to do so.

Hard answer: You couldn't sell them on "yes" – they sold you on "no."

And the appointment is the fulcrum point of the sale – you can't sell squat without a face-to-face or phone-to-phone appointment with a decision maker.

NOTE WELL: "This looks great, let me share this with my boss," is a statement that signals you have just wasted your time. And in my opinion is NOT an appointment. That is visiting.

An appointment is when you meet with someone to further the sales process or you meet with someone who can decide.

RED WHINE ...

"The guy won't give me an appointment."

What do you have to do to change in order to achieve or exceed your sales appointment objectives?

Create some compelling reasons beyond the feeble ones you now use – saving money, five minutes of your time, I'll be in the neighborhood tomorrow, gather some information, and other puke.

AND stop blaming other people for your lack of sales skills. Now – some of you make appointments and sell over the phone – some

make appointments and go outside to sell –
some make appointments at events – and all
of you think "my way is different, Jeffrey" –
and you are wrong – all appointment setting
is the same – engage a qualified decider and
get them to commit to your presentation.

Don't sell the product.

Don't sell the service.

Sell the appointment.

They can't push a
contract or a check
through the phone
– just sell the appointment.

How do you get an appointment?

You ask. Well, not quite. You engage,
you spark, you provide value, you interest,
you create desire.

If you call and the person is willing, and
you set the appointment, that's dumb luck.
My five-year-old granddaughter Morgan
can mail out information and set an
appointment with someone who's willing.
This is about the people who perceive
they're not.

**RED SELLING
RESPONSE ...**

"If all you have
is a product or
a service no
one will meet
with you. If
you have a
profit driven
answer,
everyone
will meet
with you."

Major clue: If they have no interest, you will not get the appointment. If you provide no perceived value, they will not appoint you. If you are not engaging, they will not appoint you. If they PERCEIVE they have no need, they will not appoint you.

You need to build your expertise beyond your brochure and your price list. Instead of studying TV at night, you need to become an expert in the industry or categories you cover, you need to know where your prospect or customer uses your product or service to build their business and make a profit

RED WHINE ...

"He made an appointment and didn't show."

As a result you may need to become an expert in branding, customer loyalty, use of media, customer response, delayed response, publicity, public relations, converting responses to sales, image building, and EVERY element that the customer is seeking as he or she plans THEIR sales campaign, or their business.

None of this appears in your literature. If you want to know the effectiveness of your current brochure, grab a red Sharpie and circle ALL the areas that your customer or prospect would consider valuable or save-able.

The first thing you gotta do BEFORE you ever get the appointment is get the attention and interest of the DECISION MAKER. You do this by engaging him or her and you engage with questions or statements that lead to their wanting to know more. And not necessarily more about you – rather more about what you know that could help them.

> You have to know
> something about them.
>
> You have to be brief.
>
> You can't sell more than
> an appointment.
>
> Don't ask, "How are you today?"
> or "Have you ever heard of us?"

You engage – the heart of the appointment process is the engagement.

RED SELLING RESPONSE ...
"Are they looking forward to your meeting? Or are you a necessary evil?"

Ask compelling and engaging questions.
When I sold lists of new corporations and new homeowners, I would walk into a potential customer and ask, "Who's in charge of sales leads?" That question got me an appointment more than 50% of the time. If you sell copiers or you're a printer, ask, "Who's in charge of image?" or, if you're an accountant or a banker, ask, "Who's in charge of profits?"

THE DECISION MAKER

Ask the prospect what they think. And tell the prospect how he wins or could win by meeting with you. Do not save the prospect money – earn the prospect profit. Ask for a short time with an option to make longer if interested.

Start higher on the decision-making chain than you dare.

If you're thinking, "Should I go to the accounting department or the office manager?" NO! – Go to the CEO.

Talk profit and productivity – NOT SAVING MONEY – talk ideas and opportunities – NOT A CHANCE TO TELL YOU WHAT I DO – they want friendly, help, answers, productivity, and profit.

It's not a benefit statement. It's a profitability statement.
It's not a benefit statement. It's a productivity statement.

THEY DO NOT WANT TO BE OR NEED TO BE EDUCATED. They want answers just like you do. THEY DO NOT WANT SOLUTIONS. They want answers. THEY DO NOT WANT TO TAKE THEIR TIME TO HEAR ABOUT YOU. If they give you time, it better be about them.

Which do you think a prospect wants, answers to their problems or your sales pitch?

Offer answers as a reason to meet, and presto!
The appointment is yours.

Free Red Bit: Want a lesson in persistence? Go to www.gitomer.com, register if you are a first time user, and enter the word PERSISTENCE in the RedBit box.

Will the real decision maker please stand up.

The prospect tells you, "I only need one more approval and the order is yours." – *For joy, for joy – the order is mine!* – Eh, eh, eh – don't celebrate too soon. The one last person needed to approve is the real decision maker. The boss. The guy you were supposed to be talking to in the first place. The one person who can say "no," and there's no possibility of reversing it. Rut-row.

Throw some water on yourself, pal. This sale hangs by a thread – and what are you doing about it? Going home and bragging "it's in the bag," or saying over and over – "I hope I get it, I hope I get it?" Neither will work.

Here's what to do: The words "I only need one more approval and the order is yours" must trigger your response to the prospect – "Great, when do we all meet?" Get the prospect to agree to let you attend the final decision meeting.

If you're not present when
the last decision is made
– odds are you will lose
the final battle of the sales war
without being able
to fire one bullet.

THE DECISION MAKER

Try this: (In a non-salesy, friendly way), say to the prospect, "I'm an expert at (what you do), and, Mr. Jones, you're an expert at (what they do). Surely, as you discuss our service, questions about productivity and profitability will arise. I'm sure you agree that the right information needs to be presented so that the most intelligent decision can be made, true? (get commitment) And questions might arise about our service. I'd like to be there to answer questions about my expertise so you can make a decision that's in the best interest of your business." (If this fails, try adding on the phrase – "Pleeeeaaase, I'll be your best friend.")

RED WHINE ...

"Now they need a proposal."

If the prospect (customer) agrees to the meeting, he or she considers you a resource, a partner. They trust you. If they don't agree to let you in the meeting – they just consider you a salesperson.

When others need to "final approve" the deal,

besides learning to qualify the buyer better, you must take these five action steps or the sale is in jeopardy ...

1. Get the prospect's personal approval.
"Mr. Prospect, if it was just you, and you
didn't need to confer with anyone else, would
you buy?" (The prospect will almost always
say yes.) Then ask, "Does this mean you'll
recommend our service to the others?" Get
the prospect to endorse you and your service
to the others, but don't let him (or anyone)
make your pitch for you.

2. Get on the prospect's team. Begin to
talk in terms of "we," "us," and "the team."
By getting on the prospect's team, you can
get the prospect on your side of the sale.

3. Arrange a meeting with all deciders.
Do it any (ethical) way you have to.

4. Know the prime decider in advance.
"Tell me a little bit about the others."
(Write down every characteristic.) Try to get
the personality traits of the other deciders.

**5. Make your entire presentation
again.** You only have to do this if you want
to make the sale. Otherwise just leave it to
the prospect. He thinks he can handle it on
his own, and will try his best to convince
you of that.

If you think you can get around these
five steps, think again. (It's obvious
you're looking for shortcuts or you would
have properly qualified the buyer in the
first place.)

**RED SELLING
RESPONSE ...**
"Decision
makers
don't need
proposals
if you present
a compelling,
value or
profit driven
proposition."

If you make the mistake of letting your prospect become a salesperson on your behalf (goes to the boss or group instead of you), you will lose. Most every time.

Here are 2.5 ounces of prevention (for next time):

1. Qualify the decision maker as the "only" by asking a seemingly innocent question at the beginning of your presentation – "Is there anyone else you work with (confer with, bounce things off of) on decisions (situations) like this?" The object is to find out if anyone else is involved in the decision BEFORE you make your presentation.

2. Prevent the situation from occurring by saying in your initial presentation: "If you're interested in our _____, when we're finished, would it be possible to meet the CEO and chat about it?"

2.5 The most powerful qualifying question you can ask is (AND IT MUST BE ASKED EXACTLY THIS WAY): *"Bill, how will this decision be made?" Bill will give you an answer. AND YOU FOLLOW UP WITH THE QUESTION: "Then what?" And Bill will begin to give you the saga about how the decision is really made. You ask "then*

RED WHINE ...

"He said they spent their whole budget."

what?" four or five times and PRESTO!, you'll have the name of the real decision maker.

The number of sales you make will be in direct proportion to the number of actual decision makers you sit in front of. The problem with most salespeople (not you of course) is that they are sitting in front of someone who has to ask their mommy or daddy if they can buy it or not.

Real salespeople sit in front of real decision makers. How real are you?

RED SELLING RESPONSE ...

"Decision makers make the budget. Non-decision makers spend the budget."

Free Red Bit: Want to have a few reasons why people don't decide? It will give you a bit better insight to their (and your) decision-making process. Go to www.gitomer.com, register if you are a first time user, and enter DECIDE in the RedBit box.

Decision maker won't give you an appointment? You suck!

And all these years, you've been blaming it on somebody else.

THE DECISION MAKER

Red♠Bites

Can't get past the gatekeeper? You suck! It never ceases to amaze me how many salespeople will whine to me that they couldn't get past the gatekeeper. How many times do you have to get hit over the head with a hammer before you finally decide this isn't working. If you can't get past the gatekeeper, why don't you simply create a different approach? My first recommendation is, don't go to the gatekeeper. Stand out in the parking lot and ask anyone besides the gatekeeper and they will help you. But there's a secret to getting past the gatekeeper every time. And I'm going to share it with you now so that you can use it forever. Go up to the gatekeeper and ask for someone in sales. A salesperson will appear in under three minutes ready to tell you everything about everyone. That's the job of salespeople, tell people things. They will lead you to the CEO and as you're walking down the hallway they will tell you the kind of car he drives, what college he attended, the name of his children, his favorite sports team and his golf handicap. He will reveal all the secrets of the company and will do so gladly.

RED WHINE ...

"The guy said he had to talk it over with ..."

That's the secret. Ask for someone in sales. And then make your request of him or her.

 Can't get your voicemail returned? You suck! Everyone has a voicemail strategy and very few of them work. One of the reasons is that voicemail screens out unwanted calls and unwanted people. You may be among the unwanted. Certainly you're among the unknown. In *The Sales Bible*, there's a strategy of leave half a message, pretend like you're cut off and hang up. Go get *The Sales Bible*. In my seminars I tell people to have their kid leave a message when someone persistently will not return your call. If you use the kid message it will be returned in 20 minutes, guaranteed. But the object of voicemail is to use it to convey some kind of valuable reason to get a call returned, or it won't get returned. That's not a difficult concept to understand. If you give someone a proposal and leave a voicemail saying, "I hope you got my proposal, if you have any questions call me," that voicemail is not going to get returned. Because it's stupid. You know it's stupid, I know it's stupid, and the customer knows it's stupid. The secret to voicemail is be slightly daring and take risks. If you're humorous and creative you've got a shot at it, if you're not you don't.

RED SELLING RESPONSE ...

"Decision makers don't need to talk it over with anyone."

THE DECISION MAKER

Principle 7

ENGAGE ME AND YOU CAN MAKE ME CONVINCE MYSELF

- **Ask the wrong questions. Get the wrong answers.**
- **Ask smart questions, they think you're smart.**

RedBites

- Asking powerful questions will make prospects think in new ways.
- What you ask sets the tone and the perception of the buyers.
- What you ask determines their response.
- What you ask makes or breaks the sale.
- Your questions are a critical factor in the way your customers perceive you.

"REMEMBER, YOU CAN'T JUST WALTZ IN AND SELL SOMETHING. FIRST YOU'VE GOT TO LICK HIS FACE FOR A FEW MINUTES!"

Ask the wrong questions.
Get the wrong answers.

The most important aspect of making a sale –
is also a major weakness of every salesperson.
Asking questions.

It's an enigma to me. Questions are so critical, you'd think it would be the topic of training every week. Yet salespeople are odds on favorites to have never taken one training program in the science of asking a question.

How critical? The first personal (rapport) question sets the tone for the meeting, and the first business question sets the tone for the sale. That's critical. Benefits of asking the right question? Good question.

Here are 9.5 benefits to make sales by:
1. Qualify the buyer.
2. Establish rapport.
3. Create prospect disparity.
4. Eliminate or differentiate from the competition.
5. Build credibility.
6. Know the customer and their business.
7. Identify needs.
8. Find hot buttons.
9. Get personal information.
9.5 Close the sale.

All these answers come from asking the right questions. Power Questions.

Here's the rub:
Do you have 25 of them – the most powerful questions you can create – at your fingertips? No? Join the crowd. 95% of all salespeople don't. That could be why only 5% of salespeople rise to the top. Just a theory (or is it?).

Here's the challenge:
Get every prospect and customer to say "No one ever asked me that before."

RED WHINE ...
"The prospect just sat there."

Here are the 7.5 questioning success strategies:

1. Ask prospect questions that make him evaluate new information.

2. Ask questions that qualify needs.

3. Ask questions about improved productivity, profits or savings.

4. Ask questions about company or personal goals.

5. Ask questions that separate you from your competition – not compare you to them.

6. Ask questions that make the customer or prospect think before giving a response.

7. **Ask Power Questions to create a BUYING atmosphere** – not a selling one.

7.5 A critical success strategy: To enhance your listening skills, write down answers. It proves you care, preserves your data for follow-up, keeps the record straight, and makes the customer feel important.

How do you formulate a power question?
Here's the secret:
There's a secret to creating and asking the right type of Power Question. A question that makes them think (and respond) about me in terms of the prospect.

Sounds complicated – but it isn't.
Here are some bad examples:
• What type of life insurance do you have?
• Do you have a pager?
• Who do you currently use for long distance service?
All stink.

Here are some good examples:
• If your husband died, how would the house payments be made? How would the children go to college?
• If your most important customer called right now, how would you get the message?
• If your long distance charges were

RED SELLING RESPONSE ...
"If you ask compelling questions it's impossible for the prospect to just sit there."

30% higher than they should be, how would you know?

All make the buyer think and respond in terms of his own interests, and answer in terms of the seller. WOW!

Here's a winner:
Scott Wells, of Time Warner Cable in Raleigh, came up with a grand-slam home-run question in training session – The objective was to ask a prospect qualifying questions about getting cable TV, and sell all premium channels possible. Scott asked "If you owned your own cable channel, Ms. Jones, what would be on it?" WOW, what a question – it draws out all the likes (and perhaps the dislikes) of the customer, and puts every answer in terms of the sale being made.

Here's a series:
Let's say I train sales teams (hey, what a coincidence, I do). Here's a series of questions designed to make my prospect think about himself, and answer in terms of me. (Answers are not given here, and can sometimes play a part in question order, but you'll get the process.)

RED WHINE ...
"He kept interrupting me with phone calls."

• How many of your salespeople did not meet their sales goals last year?

• Why? (What was the major cause?)

• What plans have you made to ensure that they will this year?

• What type of personal development plan for each salesperson have you put into place?

• How do you support your sales staff?

• How much training did you budget last year?

• How much did you wish you'd have budgeted?

• When training takes place, how do you measure each individual's professional development progress?

These eight questions will give me enough answers to rewrite their sales record book (and their checkbook).

It's not just asking questions, it's asking the right questions. A sale is made or lost based on the questions you ask. If you aren't making all the sales you want – start by evaluating the specific wording of the questions you're asking. Your answers are in your questions.

Questions unlock sales.
Uh, any questions?

RED SELLING RESPONSE ...

"If your message is impactful, the prospect will "hold his calls."

Looking for a few Power Question lead-ins? Try these...

- *"What do you look for ...?"*

- *"What have you found ...?"*

- *"How do you propose ...?"*

- *"What has been your experience ...?"*

- *"How have you successfully used ...?"*

- *"How do you determine ...?"*

- *"Why is that a deciding factor ...?"*

- *"What makes you choose ...?"*

- *"What do you like about ...?"*

- *"What is one thing you would improve about ...?"*

- *"What would you change about ...?" (Do not say, "What don't you like about ...?")*

  - *"Are there other factors ...?"*

  - *"What does your competitor do about ...?"*

  - *"How do your customers react to ...?"*

RED WHINE ...

"He said he wasn't interested."

To use questions successfully, they must be thought out and written down in advance. Develop a list of 15 to 25 questions that uncover needs, problems, pains, concerns, and objections. Develop 15 to 25 more that create prospect commitment as a result of the information you have uncovered.

Practice. After about 30 days of asking the right questions you'll begin to see the real rewards.

Ask smart questions, they think you're smart. Ask dumb ...

Sales Truth: Salespeople become known by the questions they ask.

Knowing this truth, you'd think all salespeople would ask smart questions. You'd be thinking wrong. It never ceases to amaze me, that with all the options salespeople have, they choose to alienate, anger or cause doubt in the mind of the prospect by setting the wrong tone with their questions.

RED SELLING RESPONSE ...

"If the prospect isn't interested, it's because you were not interesting."

*Here are the dumbest questions salespeople ask –
and why they're dumb:*

• **Who are you currently using …?**
Pre-call research should tell you that. And maybe the prospect
feels that's none of your business. Good start.

• **Are you satisfied with your present …?** Everyone will
tell you they're satisfied. So what? Well, OK, if you're satisfied,
I'll just leave and quit.

• **How much are you currently paying for …?** None of
your business #2. Let's get down to price as fast as you can.

• **Can I quote you on …?** Why send a quote – the next person
who quotes 2¢ cheaper gets the business. What about the value?

• **Can I bid on …?** Same as a "quote" only worse. This is a 100%
price driven sale. Low margin. Low profit. Low commission. Low
percentage of success. How low do you want to go?

• **Tell me a little bit about your business?** No. It's a waste
of the prospect's time. Find out a little bit about the prospect's
business so you can go into the sales call with answers and
ideas that may get the prospect excited enough to buy.

• **Are you the person who decides about …?** Come on.
This is THE question that breeds the most lies. The answer is
most often "yes," and the answer most often is false. Why ask a
question that breeds misleading information? The correct
question to ask is: How will the decision be made?

• **If I could save you some money, would you …?** Every
salesperson thinks that the customer will jump at the hint of
saving money. This tactic actually has a negative effect on the
buyer and makes the salesperson work twice as hard to prove
himself and usually at a lower price (and lower commission).

And the worst question of them all:

• **What would it take to get (earn) your business?**
This question literally is saying to the prospect: "Look, I don't have much time here. Could you just tell me the quickest way to get this order, and make me do the least amount of work possible to get it."

DUMB WORDS: Let's add a bunch of negative words that prospects hate or gets their guard up – today, frankly, honestly, if I were you, or anything negative about the previous choice they made or anything negative about your competition.

Now, before you get all hostile on me, I'm not saying don't get this information. I am saying there are smarter, better ways of getting this information that will lead you to a sale. The questions above make the prospect have a lower opinion of you, and that will lead to nothing but price wars and frustration.

These are all "price driven questions." In other words they are the kind of questions where the sale boils down to the price. And if you want the sale real bad – simple, just lower your price to where you make little or no profit. Duh.

The secret of good (smart) questions are those that make the prospect stop and think, and answer in terms of you. If you ask people questions that you could have found out the answer by some means as simple as looking up the information on their web site, how intelligent or hard working does that make you look? Not very.

NOTE: You do have the luxury of asking a weak question about their stuff, if you preface it with the statement, "I was looking at your web site last night and I got a couple of ideas I'd like to talk to you about, but there were a few things I'd like to understand a little better about the way you serve your customer." NOW YOU CAN ASK ANYTHING AND STILL LOOK SMART.

If you walk in with an IDEA that you got from reading their annual report, their trade magazine, or reading their web info, you will earn the respect of the person making the buying decision. You will also be viewed as credible. Respect and credibility lead to trust. Trust leads to sale. Think about that the next time you're formulating a question.

The sale is yours for the asking; all you gotta do is ask for it in the right way.

Free Red Bit: Want a few real smart questions? Well, since everyone sells something different, I'll give you the lead-ins to the questions and you adapt it to whatever you sell. Fair enough? Go to www.gitomer.com, register if you are a first time user, and enter the words SMART QUESTIONS in the RedBit box.

Red Bites

Asking powerful questions will make prospects think in new ways. That's the bold part. You ask questions to get prospects to give you information that will lead you closer to the sale. You want information that affected prospects in the past, so you want to find out about their past experiences. You want to understand their motives for buying. And – you want to find out what criteria they used in selecting you. To get prospects to think in new ways, you have to ask thought-provoking questions. Here's a good example: "Mr. Jones, what would you do if you lost two of your top 10 customers?" That question is followed with, "What's your plan to keep them loyal?" Now, those are questions that don't have a specific product or service behind them. They may not fit everyone's business, but baby, they are thought provoking. You might want to ask yourself the same questions.

What you ask sets the tone and the perception of the buyers. When you begin a question with the phrase "What's been your experience with …?" prospects turn into wisdom providers instead of information providers. Instead of giving them your wisdom, buyers will like you a whole lot more when you ask for their wisdom. Unfortunately, salespeople think they have to "educate" buyers. Nothing could be further from the truth. Buyers don't want an education. Buyers want answers. Your questions set the stage for the selling process – which is really the buying process. Your job is to set the buying tone by engaging the prospect intellectually and emotionally.

What you ask determines their response. If you're looking to get into a battle about why your product is different from the competition's product – or why your price is higher – just ask a dumb question about how the competition is treating the customer. If you ask a question about bidding or saving money, your answers are going to be in terms of "price" and "what kind of deal can you give me?" But if you ask value questions – questions about productivity and profit – you're going to get answers that lead you to your prospects' motives for buying.

What you ask makes or breaks the sale. If you know that questions are critical, why are you spending more time watching TV reruns than developing new questions? (NOTE: I just asked you a value question.) If you know that questions are critical, why don't you have a list of 25 questions that your competition is not asking? The more thought provoking your questions, the more your prospective buyers will respect you. The higher that respect level is, the more likely they are to be truthful with you and give you insight into the key factors that will determine the sale. They will also begin to share the truth about how the decision is made. Every minute you're in front of prospects they're deciding how much they like you, how much they believe you, how much they respect you, how much confidence they have in you, and how much they trust you. All of these factors determine whether or not they will buy from you.

Your questions are a critical factor in the way your customers perceive you. If they're intelligent and engaging, they consider you a person of value. If your questions are dumb, they consider you a salesperson of price.

"DO YOU REALIZE I'LL GET FIRED IF YOU DON'T BUY SOMETHING?
CAN YOU LIVE WITH YOURSELF IF THE BANK TAKES MY HOUSE AND MY
CHILDREN HAVE TO SELL THEIR TOYS ON E-BAY? HOW WILL YOU FEEL
WHEN OUR POODLE STARTS EATING PEOPLE TO SURVIVE?"

It's not hard sell, it's heart sell.

Good questions get to the heart
of the problem/need/situation
very quickly – without the buyer
feeling like he or she
is being pushed.

– Jeffrey Gitomer

Principle 8

IF YOU CAN MAKE THEM LAUGH, YOU CAN MAKE THEM BUY!

- Having the first laugh makes a sale that lasts.
- Need to improve your humor? Become a student of humor.

Red中Bites

- Humor. The final frontier.
- Humor is the highest form of language mastery.
- What's so funny about being professional?
- The difference between a joke and a story.
- Laughter is universal.

"GETTING A CUSTOMER TO LAUGH IS A GOOD THING. HOWEVER,
FIRING UP A BONG IN HIS OFFICE MIGHT NOT BE THE BEST WAY ..."

Having the first laugh makes a sale that lasts.

Hey, I got a new photo. It's about time – the other one was four years old. I've lost a bit of hair since the last one – OK, OK I've lost a lot of hair since the last one. But I couldn't tell – they fell out one at a time.

There are two ways of looking at my hair loss.

1. **Oh, my gosh, I'm losing my hair -- woe is me.**

2. **There's not much more to lose.**

I have tried to use my misfortune (if you want to look at the vain side) as an opportunity to poke fun at myself and make others laugh.

For example in a seminar I'll say, "I'm not actually losing my hair – I'm a hair donor. I give my hair to people less fortunate than myself." – and I'll point to someone with lots of hair. And I'll add, "The Hair Club for Men refused to let me join. They said you have to have some to get in."

Or I'll say, "I wear great ties, because I know no one is ever going to come up to me and say – 'Jeffrey – Great hair!'" The hair thing has been beneficial financially – for example, I use very little shampoo – and even less conditioner. It takes me very little time to comb my hair – giving me lots of time to work on other beauty areas.

Last week someone wanted me to describe myself so I could be met at the plane. I said, "I'm six feet tall, weigh about 185, have a beard, my hair is short – and some of it's missing (my customer howled with laughter).

The other day in Dallas I needed a haircut and was in one of those snazzy hotels. I figured "how expensive can it be?" and went ahead without asking the price. Fifty bucks, they charged. I asked the guy, "What is it – a dollar a hair?"

RED WHINE ...

"The guy had no sense of humor."

Well the humor thing seems destined to be in my presentation material, because the hair thing definitely is not. What's your humor point? Do you have one?

The Major Clue: Making people smile or laugh puts them at ease and creates an atmosphere more conducive for agreement. If they agree with your humor, they are more likely to agree with purchasing your product or service.

• **Pick something that's funny to you.** The lack of hair used to bug me – now it doesn't (as much). Now I look for ways to laugh about it – because I can't change it.

• **Pick something that's personal to you.** If it's about you, it's comfortable to you.

- **Develop lines that are tested to make people laugh -- nothing corny.** Try out the lines on your friends and co-workers first. If they laugh – use them. If they groan, so will everyone else.

- **Keep the lines clean. Real clean.**

- **Be careful about ethnic or gender.** My recommendation is – don't.

- **Poke fun at yourself.** It's OK if the finger points at you. It's NOT OK if you make fun at the expense of others.

- **Don't drag it out.** Use it once or twice and move on.

- **Take small humor risks** – If the other guy is bald, I say – "You know, the first thing I liked about you was your hair." He laughs and we grow a bit closer having a "plight-in-common."

I believe that making people smile is a major key in selling. The prospect may not be interested in hearing about your stuff, but they're always looking to smile or laugh.

Want some safe topics?

- **Children** (What they did or said.)

- **Traffic** (What you did or saw.)

- **Repeating a sit-com or television line** (With acknowledgments to the source.)

RED SELLING RESPONSE ...
"Don't tell jokes, tell stories."

- **Self-stuff** (Hair, clothes, make-up, shoes.)

- **Self-abilities** (Golf, tennis, running, exercise.)

- **Self-improvement** (Frustrations climbing the ladder or studying.)

Developing humor takes time. Like all other sales skills, it must be learned. And, yes, some people are "naturally funnier" than others. BUT if you're not very funny, you can learn. The best way I've found is to pay attention to what happens to you.

RED WHINE ...

"My Powerpoint slides are boring."

The other day I was in the shower in a hotel and broke open a new bottle of hair shampoo. After I used it and put the lid back on, I remarked to myself, "You know you don't have much hair when you use the shampoo and you can't tell any is missing." I laughed at myself. Do you?

Humor not only helps make the sale – it also helps build the relationship. Laughter is mutual approval, and mutual approval is at the fulcrum point of selling. If you can make them laugh, you can make them buy.

"But Jeffrey, I'm not a funny person," you say. "My sense of humor is about zero." – So? Go study humor.

MAKE 'EM LAUGH

Free Red Bit: Want a list of things you can do to be more humorous? Go to www.gitomer.com, register if you are a first time user, and enter the word HUMOR in the GitBit box.

May the joke be with you …

"I STARTED MY SALES PRESENTATION WITH A COUPLE OF STORIES AND THEY ALL LAUGHED THEIR ASSES OFF … TOO BAD I'M NOT SELLING ASSES!"

RED SELLING RESPONSE …

"Powerpoint is used to convey a message. Powerpoint humor is an acceptable messenger."

Need to improve your humor? Become a student of humor.

1. Visit comedy clubs. Study delivery and timing. Watch audience reaction. Observe what makes them laugh. What makes you laugh?

2. Watch comedy shows on TV/cable. The older shows tend to be funnier. Make a note of what's funny. Bugs Bunny is funny. Actions, vocal tones, facial expressions, words, types of stories.

RED WHINE ...

"I'm a professional salesperson. I don't have to be funny."

3. Read joke books, or books that are funny. Milton Berle's joke book is particularly good. Books written by humorists like Dave Barry, Art Buchwald, Scott Adams, and Lewis Grizzard are great.

4. Join Toastmasters. They have advanced programs in humorous speaking.

5. Watch and listen to children very carefully. Kids are naturally funny in both words and actions.

6. Read history. The truth is often stranger and funnier than fiction.

7. Take humor risks where you don't have much to lose – at home, with friends, in divorce court, in prison, etc.

8. Take a professional comedian or joke writer to lunch. You will learn the make-up of humor by spending time with professionals.

9. Practice making funny faces and gestures in the mirror. If you're really brave, use the rear view mirror.

10. Get out your high school yearbook. Talk about funny – look up your picture. Or your girlfriend's.

11. Take an acting class. This is a good way to come out of your shell. A friend of mine told me that I was acting like a jerk. I told him I wasn't acting.

12. Carry audiotapes of your favorite comedians with you in the car. Pop them in before you make a sales call to get a lift.

13. Start looking for humor in your everyday life. Try to appreciate it as it is happening, instead of always in hindsight.

14. Practice exaggerating your gestures and experimenting with your posture. A lot of humor is body language humor. Learn to be funny without saying a word.

15. Hang around funny people. It's amazing how your humor will increase when you're in the company of people who are funny.

RED SELLING RESPONSE ...

"Professional salespeople tend to lose to friendly salespeople. Don't take my word for it, ask any good old boy."

15.5 Laugh a lot. If you're serious about using humor, start smiling and laughing more.

Red  Bites

Humor is the final frontier. It's easy to learn all about your product, it's easy to learn all about your customer, it's easy to learn the science of selling, it's hard to learn the science of humor and harder to learn how to place that humor and time that humor into your sales presentation. The essence of humor is that it is relaxing and creates a more open atmosphere. An atmosphere that will begin to breed friendship, respect and compatibility. The reason I refer to it as the final frontier is that it's the last element that you put into your selling process.

> You use humor when
> you're the master of
> knowing your own product,
> knowing your customer
> and his business,
> and knowing the science of selling.

If you only use humor and don't know the other three elements, then you will be a clown who makes no sales. Humor will not "get you by," rather it will solidify your relationship, and the sale.

MAKE 'EM LAUGH

Humor is the highest form of language mastery.
If you've ever heard someone say, "Boy, that guy's just naturally funny," he's also probably an extremely intelligent human.
If you ever learn a foreign language, the very last thing you do is learn the humor. The hardest thing to do in any foreign language is make a joke. Humor is the most difficult of nuances to master, but when you do, you have the basis for solid intellectual rapport and solid intellectual engagement. NOTE WELL: Not every prospect requires or desires humor. You can tell who they are right away. They're the ones that never laugh at anything. The best thing to do when this scenario occurs is eliminate humor from your sales presentation and pray the guy is not a price buyer. In my experience though, he probably is. People who "just want to get down to brass tacks," are usually just people who want to "get down to brass prices."

What's so funny about being professional?
If your entire sales talk is professional, you are likely to lose to someone whose talk is 50% professional and 50% friendly, combined with funny. Friendly and funny are a thousand times more engaging than professional. If you doubt that, take a look at any latenight TV host. Are they professional or funny? How much are they making? How much are you making? I don't mean to compare your sales presentation to a David Letterman monologue, but I am going to compare the way you think you have to present versus the way your prospective buyer would like to be presented to. I have incorporated sales talk with funny talk for the last 30 years and not only has it made me a ton of sales, it has also made me a ton of friends. It will do the same for you.

The difference between a joke and a story.

Most salespeople reduce themselves to joke tellers, or should I say, joke re-tellers, or should I say bad joke re-tellers. Joke telling is dangerous, and usually not very funny. First of all, most jokes are demeaning to one person or another. Second of all, jokes sound contrived, almost like you're trying too hard. And worst of all, if the customer has heard the joke before, it makes you look like a complete idiot, especially at the end when you're the only one laughing. Stories on the other hand are genuine. They tell about experience, they can use self-effacing humor, and they're engaging. Often times when you tell a story, it makes the prospect think of a story and will engage you back (in storytelling that's called a "topper"). If you can get a story of his or hers, that's also a rapport builder. Storytelling is also effective in your sales presentation when getting the prospect to relate to your product or service. Facts and figures are forgotten, stories are retold.

Laughter is Universal.

The use of humor in sales is almost never taught. The reason is most sales training and most sales trainers aren't that funny. I'm not saying that if you're not funny you're not valid, but I am saying that if I'm in a selling situation against you and I'm funny and you're professional, or I'm funny and you're not funny, I will win the sale more often. If you don't consider yourself a funny person, study humor or read about how to become more humorous.

You can debate
how much humor to use,
you can debate
when humor is
most affectively inserted,
you can even debate
the type of humor
that should be used.
But you cannot deny
the power of laughter
as a universal bond
from human to human,
and from human
to sales order form.

– Jeffrey Gitomer

Principle 9

USE CREATIVITY TO DIFFERENTIATE AND DOMINATE

- Where does creativity come from? You baby!
- Three areas to make a difference.
- Fix your voice message now!

RedBites

- Creativity is a science that you can learn.
- A creative approach to ending "we're satisfied with our present supplier" forever.

"JUST BECAUSE IT SELLS BURGERS, I'M NOT SURE 'RONALD MᶜTOILET'
IS THE BEST WAY TO SELL INDUSTRIAL PLUMBING SUPPLIES!"

Where does creativity come from? You, baby!

"That's a great idea!"
"Did you think of that?"
"How did you think of that?"

Typical comments you might hear if you come up with a great idea. So, how DID you think of it? "I dunno, it just came to me!" you say. Well, almost. There are reasons for creativity.

People accuse me of being "creative" (among other things). So much so that I'm starting to teach others. Which is pretty cool considering I'm still a student myself.

How much do you study creativity? Answer: Not enough. Seeing a great idea is one thing – HAVING a great idea is another. Big difference between the guy that invented the pet rock and the guy that bought one. One (the inventor) is a lot more fulfilled (wealthier) than the purchaser (you).

Where does creativity come from?
You learn it.
How important is creativity in sales success?
Very.
How creative are you?
Not very.
Can you improve your creativity?
Yes. Read a book on it. Practice it.

Well, in my quest to understand the roots of personal creativity, I've questioned myself and studied my environment to come up with the elements of what drives and or inspires my own creative process. I'm not telling you this is the be-all-end-all of the creative mind, but it is an introspective look at someone who on more than one occasion has been accused of being creative. As you listen, please rate yourself on each element to see how high you are on the "creative-capable" scale.

Here are the 13.5 elements that drive and/or inspire my creative process.

RED WHINE ...

"I'm not a very creative person."

1. Brains. Stupid people aren't very creative. The smarter you are, the more likely it is that you will have (or are at least capable of having) smart, bright ideas. (All you need to do is understand where ideas come from, and how to create the atmosphere to make them happen.)

2. Attitude. Negative attitude blocks creative thought. Ever finish an argument with someone, five minutes later you think of what you could or should have said? Of course. Everyone has. The reason you didn't say it in the heat of the argument, is that your creative attitude brainwave was blocked by your negative attitude brainwave.

3. The habit of observing. Looking at things and circumstances is one thing. Seeing an idea within them is another. When something goes wrong or something goes right, those are both opportunities to think and see in terms of yourself. Two word lesson: pay attention.

4. The habit of collecting ideas.
The second you think of something that has the least amount of creativity attached to it, document it. Write it down on a napkin, your Palm Pilot, a piece of paper, or your computer. Try to expand the thought as much as you can the moment you get it. One of the most amazing and frustrating elements of life is how quickly creative ideas come and go.

5. Your self belief. In order for a greater amount of ideas to flow you must first believe you have the capability of creating one, If you tell yourself you are creative, more creative things will happen. Don't think that saying, "I am a creative person" is bragging. Look at it rather as an affirmation, telling yourself that new ideas are always on the horizon, and/or on the tip of your tongue.

USE CREATIVITY

RED SELLING RESPONSE ...
"Creativity is a learned science. Read a book on it."

6. A support system. Surround yourself with people who encourage you. The more you hear, "it'll never work," the more you'll believe it – and vice-versa. You need people around to tell you that your ideas are good. Of course, not all ideas are good. Occasionally, maybe more than occasionally, ideas will be clunkers. Maybe even borderline idiotic. Just remember at some point someone said, "I think we'll be able to fly from coast to coast in four hours," and someone else was laughing his head off. The concept, "it'll never fly," is a totally erroneous one.

RED WHINE ...
"My product is becoming a commodity."

7. The creative environment. Set your own place for creativity. Some people can operate in the noise, some people can't. Fighting environment is equally as non-productive as fighting with another human being. Both will eventually get to your attitude and impede or prevent your best ideas from springing forth. You will in fact be "impeeved" (new word).

8. Creative mentors and associations. The best way to inspire yourself is to hang around others who are creative. Someone you know casually can be just as important in your life as a mentor. The casual acquaintance may be someone who is spontaneous, creative or humorous. A mentor will be someone you can ask deeper questions of that might provide insight, and not just instant.

9. Studying creativity. The more you read, the more you will understand how others have learned and taught creativity. If you have not read the classic Michael Michalko's book *Thinkertoys*, or his new book *Cracking Creativity*, or any Edward de Bono book, *Six Thinking Hats*, *Lateral Thinking*, or a compilation of his thoughts entitled *Serious Creativity*. I recommend you start from there and immediately progress to Dr. Seuss, the champion of creativity for both adults and children. No kid can read or digest Michalko or de Bono. Every kid can read, re-read, think about, learn from, AND digest *The Cat in the Hat*, *Yertle the Turtle*, *Green Eggs & Ham*, *Horton Hears a Who*, or any of the Dr. Seuss legendary classics. My library has more than 25 volumes. OK, I've given you the titles. All you gotta do is buy them and read them.

10. Studying the history of creativity in your industry. In order for you to figure out what is going on today, and project your brilliant ideas into the future, you need to have a firm grip on what happened yesterday and why. As an expert in sales, the books I find most inspirational were written somewhere between 50 and 70 years ago. There's always a new wrinkle in something old.

RED SELLING RESPONSE ...

"If you're selling pigs or corn you've got a commodity. Anything else can be differentiated with value and creativity."

USE CREATIVITY

11. Using creative models. Look at the concepts presented in the book *Six Thinking Hats* or *Six Action Shoes*, it's a classic model in creativity where the author, Edward de Bono, uses colors of the hat or the shoe to convey a process. The easiest example of the model is a concept brought out in *Thinkertoys* called S.C.A.M.P.E.R. Scamper is simply a new way to look at an existing idea, and asking yourself questions to improve it. Each letter in the acronym represents a different perspective to see creative ideas. The letters represent Substitute, Combine, Adapt, Modify, Maximize, or Minimize, Put to other use, and Reverse or Rearrange. If you take any object, thought, or project and put the S.C.A.M.P.E.R. model to use, you will come up with new and creative ideas. The object of the model is to learn the practical science so that you can see there's a way for you to learn creativity, rather than simply be creative. Learn rather than be. One does not replace the other. One is simply an additional method or supplement to the other. Sometimes you do things or think things without really knowing "why." The "why" is never as important as the "is."

RED WHINE ...
"The customer said all copiers are alike."

12. Risk Failure. There's an old expression that says, "No risk, no reward." I say, "No risk, no nothing." All creative people take risks. It's the nature of the process. Daring to think something new or try something new. The best example of creative-failure I can give you is Thomas Edison. He's also the best example of creative-success. He thought, he studied, he tried, he risked, he failed THOUSANDS of times, and he succeeded big time. Thousands of brilliant inventions and ideas. Tens of thousands of failed ideas and inventions. Wherever your creativity takes you, risk comes along for the ride – it's a natural part of the process – enjoy the thrill of it like you would a roller coaster ride. Fail to get a hit in baseball two out of three times for 20 years and you'll go to the hall of fame with a .333 batting average.

13. Seeing your creativity in action.
There is nothing more fulfilling than seeing your idea put to use. No matter how small or grandiose people tend to brag (be proud of) and take ownership of "their idea." "See that over there? Yeah, I thought of that." Even if it's just moving something from one end of the room to the other, setting up a new configuration of the same equipment or creating a slogan, there is HUGE PRIDE in "seeing" your idea.

RED SELLING RESPONSE ...

"If your customers perceive all products to be the same, the only way to change that perception is the salesperson's ability to create a different one."

USE CREATIVITY

13.5 The ridicule factor. Whatever your great idea is, there will always be someone ready to throw cold water on it. IGNORE those people. They are jealous because they have no ideas of their own.

Now, for those of you that think all the good ideas are taken, look at the sport of ice hockey. It's more than 150 years old. The hockey (goalie) MASK is only 30 years old. Wouldn't you think that someone could have come up with it in the first 120 years? Finally one guy (Jacques Plante) got tired of getting hit in the face with the puck! Hello. And once again, necessity became the mother of invention. And he created the first hockey mask.

There are a ton of other equally obvious ideas out there – your job is to be thinking about them. There were millions of people who "knew the game" of ice hockey, but only one who imagined a better, safer way to play it.

I found a quote inscribed in the front of the book *Thinkertoys*. I have read the book several times, and ordered a case of them signed by the author, Michael Michalko. In it, he had written, 'Imagination is more important than knowledge' Albert Einstein. I rest my case. The rest is up to you.

Three Areas to Make a Difference

1. Your opening question on a sales call. Most salespeople start out with sales-puke. A bunch of info about their company and their product. Yuck. ASK A SMART QUESTION IMMEDIATELY, AND THEY'LL IMMEDIATELY THINK YOU'RE SMART.

For example …

• How much is your image worth? Do you have a specific game plan for image this year?

• How much does one lost hour of productivity cost the company? How much does it cost to lose an employee?

• If you were paying 20% more for your _____ than you had to, how would you know it?

2. Change your ordinary imaging and branding. Voice mail, fax cover sheet. List the ordinary things you do and change them today. Some other areas to get the thought process going? Your telephone greeting, your business cards, your business card title, the way you transfer a call, the way you take a message, your promotional items – and YOU!

3. Use your follow-up and "stay-in-front-of" power to the MAX. Not just the hand written thank you note. It's the Internet and your ability to have an info page – e-mail a weekly tip – create a value (testimonial stories, newsletter).

Fix your voice message now!

How do you greet your customers? Does this greeting sound familiar?

"I'm either on my phone or away from my desk."

No kidding? Pathetic.

"No, no, Jeffrey," you say. "I tell people what day it is."

"It's Monday and I'll be in meetings in the morning and I'll be in and out of the office in the afternoon."

Pathetic.

I don't care what you're doing. I called to talk to you.

Voice message is America's sales enigma. Everybody has it and 9,999 out of 10,000 have a pathetic message.

Why do I need to know that you are away from your desk? Why do I need to know that you're in a meeting? Why do I need to know what day of the week it is? Answer: I don't need to know. And more accurately. I don't want to know. What I want is to get you on the phone, that's why I called.

Many companies have two voicemail systems. One where a computer answers the phone and informs me for "my convenience" or "to serve me better" I can select from the following nine options. So by the time I reach your silly voicemail, I'm annoyed times two.

And then there's that added element of rudeness when I call and ask for you and the live attendant sends me directly to your voicemail without having the courtesy to tell me you're not there.

Pardon my rant, but what I've just given you is a solid reason for your customer to go to your competition, where their people might be friendly and more helpful.

Now let's get back to you and your stupid pathetic voicemail message. Here are 7.5 ideas to spice up your voicemail so that someone might tell someone else to call you just to hear your message. You see, people who buy your stuff talk to other people who buy your stuff. And if someone calls to hear your message that would also be known as a "lead."

Leads are expensive and hard to come by. Your voicemail is a key to getting new customers and creating word-of-mouth advertising.

1. A short message about value or profit point of your product. A hint or tip – for example tell me one thing I can do to profit from the use of your product – number them and change the message weekly

2. A thoughtful quote. The Internet will give you millions. This must be changed daily.

3. Celebrity impersonation. Find someone who does voices – or do a bad one yourself. Rodney Dangerfield "I can't get no respect – but you can get a returned phone call!"

4. Your kid. "Hi, I'm Dave's costly accident, Jason. He's out earning my college tuition. You can help by leaving a message that includes an order."

5. Something funny in general. Say this in a somewhat weary voice: "I'm just one man, and it's a big world."

6. Something funny about your product or your business: "Hi, you've reached Tom. I am out saving the world one box at a time. Please leave a message and I'll try to find a cardboard carton to save your world."

7. A testimonial from a customer. Can you imagine one of your best customers saying something like "Hi, I'm Dave Smith from ABC Plumbing. Joe is over here right now taking care of our account like he has for the past ten years. Please let him take care of yours."

7.5 Something off the wall – The reason I'm saving this for the end is that many people are uncomfortable to go off the wall and many bosses are uncomfortable by off the wall messages and sometimes the customer will not like an off the wall message. BUT, off the wall messages will be talked about the most. "Hi. I am probably here; I'm just avoiding someone I don't like. Leave me a message, and if I don't call back, it's you."

My message? – always off the wall. My present cellular phone message is: "Hi this is Jeffrey. I wish I could talk to you but I can't. Please leave your American Express card number with expiration date and I'll get right back to you." Now this may seem somewhat crazy to you, but three people a day leave their American Express number. It's fun, it's memorable, and it's non-offensive.

Make the message short. Thirty-five words maximum. Script it. Rehearse it. Then record it. Change the message often. Weekly is best. Listen to the comments carefully – they will tell you how good your message is or isn't.

If you claim to be different from your competition, a GREAT place to start is your recorded message.

"HI, I'M SUSAN FROM SUNSHINE REALTY! I HEARD YOU'RE
IN THE MARKET FOR AFFORDABLE VACATION PROPERTY ..."

Here is a list of creative voicemails some of my customers use:

"Hi you have reached Scott of RCM&D. I'm out finding new clients who have yet to realize that they need our services. Please leave me a message so that you can be the client that I am visiting."

"Hey there! It's Martin and you've called on The Greatest Day Of My Life! Thanks so much for calling and making my day even better, and please let me know who you are and what I can do to help you at the sound of the tone! Have a great day, I know I will!" ... beeeeeeep!

"Hi, this is Ray, and I'm in Nighthawk's genius training program. I'm only at the "know-it-all" level, but leave your question and I'll call you back with an answer."

"Hi, this is Randy, I wish I could talk to you but I can't. I am working like a madman to send my son away to trade school. Please leave an order and a message, and I will get back to you."

"You have reached the voicemail of Larry. I am out selling title insurance right now but please leave a message. With one daughter getting married and the other starting graduate school, you can be sure I will get back to you just as soon as I can."

I plugged my electric guitar in and strum a few really bad chords, then I come on and say, *"Hi, this is Greg. I can't come to the phone 'cause I'm out practicing my electric guitar. Leave a message … Better yet, leave an order so I can afford lessons!"*

"You've reached ABC Photography. We're not here. Now that Dave is married, he finally has a life. If you want to reach him, do his wife a favor and call his cell phone at 555-1212, or leave a message."

(My 7 year old son speaking) *"Thanks for calling Leslie. This is her son Jakeb, and I need a new Playstation game. So leave your name and number and I'll MAKE SURE she calls you back."*

Red  Bites

Creativity is a science that you can learn. If I ask you
on a scale of 1-10, how important is creativity in sales and
service? You'll answer "10." If I ask you on a scale of 1-10, how
creative YOU are, that's a different, and much lower answer.
Have you ever read a book on creativity? Probably not! It
amazes me how many people have never read a book on
creativity. Well, here's the good news: there are plenty of them
at the bookstore. The best is, *Thinkertoys* by Michael Michalko.
Buy it, read it, study it.

**A creative approach to ending "we're satisfied with
our present supplier" forever.** Ever hear the prospect tell
you, "I'm satisfied with my present supplier."? Sure you have.
How many times? Why are you still listening to it? With a little
creativity you can eliminate it forever. Here's how: When you
engage the prospect say, "Mr. Jones, I make a lot of sales calls
to prospective new customers and most of them tell me
"I'm satisfied with who we've got." Our customers are ecstatic,
getting incredible value, are more productive, and are reaping
the profits of doing business with us. Would you rather be
ecstatic and more profitable or satisfied?" The customer will
say, "ecstatic and more profitable." "GREAT," you say. "I came
here today HOPING that you were satisfied with who you've
got." Take away the objection BEFORE they have a chance to
voice it.

USE CREATIVITY

Principle 10

REDUCE THEIR RISK, AND YOU'LL CONVERT SELLING TO BUYING

- **The obvious way to sell: Eliminate the risk of buying!**
- **Replace risk with a powerful closing tool: Risk removal.**

RedBites

- The biggest barrier to a sale is the unspoken risk that a prospect perceives.
- If you eliminate risk, they will buy.
- No risk, no balls.

"SIT BACK, CLOSE YOUR EYES AND IMAGINE HOW PROUD YOU'LL FEEL KNOWING YOU CAN AFFORD TO PAY TOO MUCH FOR MY PRODUCTS!"

The obvious way to sell -- eliminate the risk of buying!

Eliminate risk and prospects are more likely to buy.
What a concept! How much simpler can selling get?

In order to harness the power of this strategy, ask yourself
these five questions as they relate to your product or sale:

1. What is the definition of risk?

2. What is the cause of risk?

3. How much risk am I asking my prospects to take when they make a purchase?

4. How do I uncover risk factors?

5. How is risk taken away, removed, or eliminated?

A risk of purchase is some mental or physical barrier, real or
imagined that causes a person to hesitate or rethink ownership.
As a salesperson your job is to identify the risk and eliminate it.

Interestingly risk is harder to identify than it is to eliminate.
What is risk to some people is a walk in the park to others.
What may seem ordinary, or of no consequence to the
salesperson, is a HUGE risk to a prospect. What may be "just
a few thousand dollars" to some, may be "Oh my God, THREE
THOUSAND DOLLARS!!" to others.

REDUCE THEIR RISK

What are the most common elements of the
risk of purchase? Here are several to think
about in the way they may go through the
mind of your prospect:

• **Financial misjudgment.** Worried about
the value of dollars spent. The risk of overpay,
or not getting my money's worth.

• **Financial risk.** Is it affordable? Am I
spending too much? Is this a budget violation
or will I lack the ability to pay?

• **I don't really need it.** What if I get it
and never use it? Do I really NEED this?
Am I risking regret?

RED WHINE ...

"The guy won't
get off the
fence."

• **I may be able to get the same thing
cheaper someplace else.** I don't want to
get it now. I want to shop around, I may be
risking overpayment.

• **Not what I pictured in my mind.** This
isn't what I really want. I'm risking getting
something I really don't want.

• **Not what I
perceived or
thought at first.**
This isn't how I
pictured it. (This
is also known as second
guessing judgment.)
I'm risking getting
the wrong thing.

• **Quality of product misjudgment.** The risk of poor performance. I'm risking this thing falling apart.

• **Service after the sale won't be there.** Will it be what I expect? Will it be there when I need it? Do I want to risk poor service?

• **Product won't perform as I expected.** The function or utilization of product is in doubt. I am risking poor performance.

• **Something better exists.** The risk that there might be a better mousetrap if I just look around a bit longer.

• **Obsolete soon after I get it.** The risk that a new model will come out the day I make my purchase (computers do this all the time).

• **Looking foolish.** The risk of making a bad/dumb choice in your own mind and in the minds of others. The risk of ridicule.

• **Salesman is lying.** The risk of non-delivery, or overstated ("not-what-he-claims-it-to-be") promises. I don't trust this guy.

• **Will someone be mad at me?** Will I get in trouble? Obvious thought patterns of buyers having trouble making a decision on their own. Do I want to risk getting yelled at for this purchase?

Risk is actually a lack of confidence, trust, and believability either in the product, the service, the company, the salesperson, or in one's self. The absence of these elements causes doubt and a rethinking of the purchase.

REDUCE THEIR RISK

REALITY: If there's a need, if there's an ability to buy, if there's not a hidden agenda (existing relationship, friend in the business, not the real decider) – then the person who hesitates is doing so for one of the following reasons …

1. Cold feet

2. Their "gut" says no

3. Fear of the unknown

4. Not enough information

4.5 Lack of confidence or trust in salesperson, company, or product.
In short – the potential risk of purchase outweighs the reward of ownership.

RED WHINE …

"He told me the board had to decide."

Here's what to do:

SUCCESS STRATEGY: Find out their tolerance for taking a risk. Some people take more risks than others. Ask about gambling. Ask about entrepreneurial risks taken before. Ask about previous purchases. Measure their tolerance and their previous experiences. Look for causes.

SUCCESS STRATEGY: Know your risks of purchase. There are less than ten. List them and have "risk removing" answers for them. List what your prospect has to lose if they buy. List the corresponding (or canceling) gains if they buy. Ask your prospect to weigh the total package – not just the weaknesses or risks.

SUCCESS STRATEGY: Identify and eliminate (or outweigh). Ask your prospect: "What's the risk?" Then ask "What's the reward?" If the risk is low, and the reward is high, then the decision is obvious.

The aspect of risk is a subtle one. Only the best of salespeople will get this concept and harness it. If you don't, there's a bigger risk: The risk that the competition is kicking your butt.

Replace Risk With a Powerful Closing Tool: **Risk Removal**

You're closing in on the purchase. You feel like you've qualified the prospect, you know you're nearly there, great presentation if you don't say so yourself, but something is still missing. There's a hesitancy and you can't quite define it.

Let me help you. The prospect feels the RISK of purchase outweighs the REWARD of ownership.

You start to hear the usual stalls like, "I'll think about it, call me back later," (The kiss of death to a teetering transaction) or the ever popular, "I have to talk this over with…" Rats.

So, what do you do? Keep selling? Not exactly – the simple answer is: Just find out where the risk is, and remove it.

What is in the way of YES? What risk element is present that I can remove to close this deal?

Here are a few "inner voice" (unstated) risk fears that might be in the way of YES:

- **I really can't afford this. I may not be able to make the payments.**

- **I'll buy it, get it home and it won't work.**

- **I'll buy it, get it home and it will look awful!**

- **I'll buy it, the boss will see my decision and explode.**

- **I'll buy it, then find out if I had looked around I could have bought it for less.**

- **I'll buy it, and never use it.**

- **I'll buy it, then some newer (better) model will come along in two weeks, and I'll be stuck with a piece of history.**

- **I'll buy it, and our employees won't like it.**

- **I'll buy it, and be out all this money when I could have done without it in the first place.**

- **I'll buy it and it will go on sale next week.**

RED WHINE ...

"He wanted to know who else was, or how long we've been using this."

Get the drift? The Risk Factors are usually both invisible and unspoken because they expose the inner guts, feelings, and thoughts of the customer.

REMEDY: You can bring up a few areas of suspicion in an effort to ameliorate and address the fear; but sometimes it takes floating a few "risk removers" to discover what the "risk barrier" might be.

Here are a few examples:

• **If you're concerned about whether or not it'll work for you after you get it home, don't worry, you can ALWAYS bring it back** (and add some peace of mind). We want you to be happy.

• **We sell lots of these to companies like yours.** But if for any reason your company doesn't like it, we offer a full refund or replacement.

• **We're so sure about our competitive pricing on this item, that we'll match any advertised or quoted price that you might discover for up to 45 days after you take delivery!**

RED SELLING RESPONSE ...

"No one wants to risk but everyone wants the reward that risk brings. You can get them off the fence, you can eliminate the board from deciding, and you can make them more comfortable by identifying and eliminating the risk elements of purchasing from you."

Please note:
If the risk is price, then the compensation is value.

REDUCE THEIR RISK

Risk is real. And a real block to a sale. And too often
salespeople misjudge risk for objection and continue to press
for the close. (Ever had a pushy salesman who seemed more
interested in your wallet than your safety?)

Risks are inner emotions that are judged and justified logically
in the mind of the prospective purchaser.

There is no "one" remedy. Sooooo, here's what to do:

1. **Identify your risks.**

2. **Create GREAT corresponding risk
   removers or even preventers.**

3. **Try them out on prospects who resist
   for no stated reason.**

4. **Master them so that your prospects
   buy more often.**

4.5 **Teach them to everyone.**

I'VE SAVED THE BEST FOR LAST: There is ONE technique
that can work to both find the risk, and close the deal.
BUT it's a delicate one that requires mastery through
preparation and practice.

The strategy is called: What's the risk? What's the reward?
When a prospect hesitates, you simply ask him or her to
list the risks of purchase. Actually write them down.
Prompt others. If the prospect says "I'm not sure," you ask,
"Could it be …" After you feel the list is complete, ask the
prospect to list the rewards. Write them down, and embellish
as much as possible without puking on the prospect.

Then eliminate the risks one by one with lead in phrases like: Suppose we could … did you know that … I think we can … Then you simply ask, "can you see any other reasons not to proceed?"

> One at a time,
> brick by brick,
> remove the risks that
> the buyer perceives
> as fatal mistakes
> in his decision-
> making process.
> Then drive home
> the rewards,
> both emotionally
> and logically.

If the customer is qualified, has a stated need, wants it – and it has become risk free, then you have the reward. The order.

Free Red Bit: Want to know three risk alarms? Three ways to determine that "risk" may be the reason for non-purchase. Sure you do. Go to www.gitomer.com, register if you are a first time user, and enter the word RISK in the RedBit box.

REDUCE THEIR RISK

Red ♠ Bites

The biggest barrier to a sale is the unspoken risk that a prospect perceives. Every time you say a word or take an action in the selling process, the prospect passes a judgment: on you and your product or service. Should I buy or should I pass? Do I like this guy? Trust this guy? Believe this guy? The prospect is weighing several factors, but the primary one is: What's the risk of buying vs. what's the reward of ownership? The secondary factor is: what's the need vs. what's the value? If the reward is high and the risk is low, if the need is high and the value is high, then the order is almost certain. The problem is that the buyer keeps this information to himself. His "hole-cards" if you play poker. And he's not gonna show them unless you "call." You put in your chips to see his cards. Once these factors are uncovered. Once he shows his cards, he has revealed his "motive to buy," the single strongest piece of sales information you can obtain. It's also the single hardest information to obtain. Keep reading ...

If you eliminate risk, they will buy. If you don't eliminate it, they will not buy, and you will not know why. So you have to ask the prospect, just like you ask for the sale. What's the risk vs. what's the reward? The secondary question to ask is: what's the need vs. what's the value? The difference (and the power) in these questions is when you ask about risk/reward, and need/value, you'll get better, more intelligent, more honest answers. They're higher level sales questions. They command respect, and will breed a higher level of mutual understanding. And those answers will lead you to the sale. Keep reading ...

No risk, no balls. "No risk, no reward," is a cliché you have heard a million times. And it's wrong. I say, "No risk, no nothing." Any salesperson who is unwilling to risk should get out of sales. Not just a risk in asking for the sale. Risk in prospecting, risk in cold calling, risk in fighting the competition, risk in creative follow-ups, and risk in sticking to your price and calling the prospect's bluff. Risk, or the risk factor, in selling permeates every aspect of the process. And people who are unwilling to take a risk usually lose to those who do. I call them "sales balls," and most salespeople (men and women) don't have them. Later this year I will be coming out with a line of sales balls. They'll come in a package of two (of course) and they'll come with complete instructions on how to use them. Until then:

Take more chances than you dare. You'll make more sales than you expect. That's the formula.

Principle 11

WHEN YOU SAY IT ABOUT YOURSELF, IT'S BRAGGING. WHEN SOMEONE ELSE SAYS IT ABOUT YOU, IT'S PROOF.

- Who will testify on your behalf?
- Take your customer with you on your next sales call.

Red🧩Bites

- Who is better at selling your product, you or your customer's testimonial?
- Testimonials are the only proof you've got.
- The most powerful person on your sales team is your customer.
- Testimonial power secret.

"THIS IS A WONDERFUL TESTIMONIAL FOR OUR PRODUCT LINE, TED!
YOU JUST CAN'T BUY THIS KIND OF PRAISE, ENTHUSIASM AND SINCERITY.
TELL YOUR MOM WE REALLY APPRECIATE IT."

Who will testify on your behalf? Your customers!

Testimonials. The single most powerful method of making a sale. And also the single most wasted resource in creating a marketing message.

Every time I see a testimonial, I read it with interest for two reasons. The first of course is to see what it says. And the second is to determine if it impacts my buying decision. Does it spur me to action? Or do I just get that "So what?" feeling.

Testimonials can sell when salespeople cannot sell.

One of the late great John Patterson's principles of selling was, "Advertising brings awareness, testimonial advertising brings customers." What he meant was an ad will brand you, but a testimonial ad can create action toward you.

When you say something about yourself it's bragging. When other people say it about you it's proof. That is the essence of the testimonial.

Take a moment before you read further and look at the written testimonials you are using. Would they make you pick the phone up and purchase? Or do they say the same old tired "They are wonderful people to do business with. I have been doing business with them for 10 years." That's a passive statement that sounds nice but doesn't have any buy-power.

TESTIMONIALS

Let me give you an example:
The great Ty Boyd founded one of the finest speaking skills and presentation skills schools in the world right here in Charlotte, N.C., called the Excellence in Speaking Institute. Thousands of people attend each year, and they love it. Ty wants to use a testimonial campaign. One of his students said:

"Wow! What a tremendous experience ... way beyond my expectations. You and ESI are the best!"

Way too general.

RED WHINE ...

"They gave me an objection I couldn't overcome."

To be most effective, testimonials need to have a specific message. General messages have little "act now" impact.

Here are some good examples:

- **I overcame my fear of speaking.**

- **I improved my skills 300% in three days.**

- **When I first saw myself on video -- I wasn't that good** (OK, I was horrible) – now I'm 1000% better – incredible program, incredible results.

- **Now I can give speeches AND lead meetings.**

• **My people actually listen to me now.**

• **Improving my speaking skills helped me upgrade my leadership skills to a new level.**

• **My speaking skills are 100% improved.**
My self confidence level is 1000% improved.

• **The butterflies have been replaced with skills for a lifetime.**

• **Don't let the price get in the way of your success.**
I invested in it, and it paid.

NOTE: Using a person's name in a testimonial is not important (unless it's a celebrity). A big company name is effective – no name needed unless it's the CEO.

What should a written testimonial say?

A written testimonial should be phrased in a way that takes away a risk or neutralizes a fear. It should be phrased in a way that shows a value benefit or a specific enhancement.

A testimonial should show action and make a call to action. "I used to use a competitor, I switched to ABC, so should you."

A testimonial should overcome an objection. "I thought their price was too high, bought it anyway, came to realize they had the best value."

A testimonial should re-enforce a claim. "I increased my productivity. I earned more profit."

A testimonial should claim a happy ending. "Ease of use. Speed of service. Now my people love to use the copier."

TESTIMONIALS

Then there is the unspoken secret of testimonials: How do you get them? The answer is the same as it is for referrals. You earn them. The difference with a testimonial is often you will have to earn them AND ask for them.

It's even OK to prompt the customer as to what you want them to say, IF what you want them to say is the truth. The only thing worse than an exaggerated testimonial is the prospect who bought from you, and found out that the testimonial was exaggerated.

RED WHINE ...
"I don't think the guy believed me."

I can make you one promise about testimonials. One iron-clad guarantee. They work.

I can also issue you this caution. They must be used in the proper manner or they lose their power. Often times salespeople use testimonials to get in the door. Obviously if that is your only way, do it. But the power of testimonial is the proof they offer at the time the customer is ready to decide. Testimonials should be used at the end of the sales cycle to dispel any doubt, reduce all risk, substantiate value, and pave the way to the order.

ACT NOW: List the ten customers who love you the most. Call them now, tell them what you need, and figure out a way to meet them for breakfast or lunch so that you can provide them some kind of value (an idea or lead), and at the same time earn your testimonial prize.

If you feel in any way awkward about asking your customer for this favor, I challenge you that your relationship with them is weak. So weak that your competition could earn the business.

Testimonials are power and proof you are what you say you are. Lack of testimonials is weakness and proof that you aren't what you say you are.

Free Red Bit: Want the 4.5 best ways to earn a testimonial? Go to www.gitomer.com, register if you are a first time user, and enter the word TESTIMONIAL in the GitBit box.

Take your best customer with you on your next sales call.

Who is the most powerful member of your sales team? A satisfied customer.

They can out-sell, out-brag, and out-prove anyone in your company including the CEO. Why? They're your testimonial. They are living proof your product or service is the best.

TESTIMONIALS

Want to take your best customers with you
on a sales call? You can if you video tape their
satisfaction. Sound too simple to be true?
Well, there is a small hitch. It has to be a
quality video. One that reflects your image,
and one that tells your story in a scripted
and meaningful way. A video with direction
and style.

"We bring our prospects and customers to
the awareness of the underlying theme and
objective of using a video as part of a sales
presentation: – 'What do you want to happen
when the video is removed from the VCR?'"
challenges Tim Butler, Vice President and Sales
Manager at Sunbelt Video in Charlotte, N.C.,
"The answer to that question is the little
known secret of a successful video."

RED WHINE ...

"I couldn't get
him to see
how my
product
was used."

"Too many businesses don't know the
elements of a successful video, or they make
videos for the wrong reasons," Butler
adds. "Video will lead you to a sale, but it
won't make the sale – that's the job of
the salesperson. There must be a smooth
transition from 'end of video' to 'next
step in the sales cycle.' Our success has
come by making videos 'on purpose' –
'for a purpose' – 'to achieve a
predetermined objective.'"

You've heard the expression "It's the
next best thing to being there." Well,

a sales video may be the best thing to being there. Here's why – videos don't forget – videos never have a bad day – and, videos always ask for the sale (if you tell them to). BUT – the video is the message – the salesperson is the messenger. Both must be present for maximum results.

Selected production tips for making your video:

• **High quality is worth it.** Spend the money to make it right.

• **The video is what you put in it.** You can create any message you want.

• **Less is more.** 5-8 minutes is optimum run time.

• **Before you begin yours, watch other people's videos -- several.** Get an idea of what you want and what you don't want.

• **Make your video real.** Be relaxed and animated.

• **Pre-select which parts (sales segments) you want to include**, and write a script before you start.

And the biggest secret – What is said about you is ten thousand times more powerful than you saying it. Let your satisfied customers tell as much of your story as you can.

RED SELLING RESPONSE ...

"Your customer can overcome any objection. Your customer can dispel any disbelief. Your customer can explain how the product is used for benefit and profit. In short your customer is better at sales than you are."

TESTIMONIALS

Here's another expression you've heard: "A picture is worth a thousand words." Here's the 21st century version of that expression: A video picture is worth a sale.

What's a video worth? Ask yourself these four questions, and the answer becomes self-evident:

1. **How much is your image worth?**

2. **What's one new customer worth?**

3. **What's a consistent sales message worth?**

4. **How much is a trained sales force worth?**

I hear companies having budget fights about whether they should have a video sales tool or not. What a joke. A bunch of non-salespeople trying to dictate the future of the company, and omitting a vital tool that will carry them to success. It's like saying "Let's buy that big boat over there – but, ah, let's not get the engine, it costs too much." DUH. If a video is not in your budget, gag (or fire) the bean counters, cut your own pay, or go into debt for it. It's that valuable.

Take your best customer with you on your next sales call. (Take them on video.)

Author's note: I made my first sales video two years ago. It cost more money than I had. Over the last 24 months it has helped me make more sales than I could count. This year I'm making a new one, and spending four times more than I spent on the first one, that I couldn't afford. And (thanks to my first video) this year, I can afford it.

Red Bites

Who is better at selling your product, you or your customer's testimonial? Not even close. Your customer can outsell you one hundred to one. And even though you intuitively know this, you still think you have to "sell" and "educate" the prospect. Nothing could be more powerful than the words of one customer who loves you, telling a customer thinking about doing business with you to DO IT! Are you going to believe your next door neighbor who just bought a car like the one you want, or a car salesman? Neighbor of course. Same with your business baby.

Testimonials are the only proof you've got.
My "testimonial mantra" for years has been: "When you say it about yourself, it's bragging. When somebody else says it about you it's PROOF!" Knowing this, you would think EVERY sales organization and salesperson would use testimonials as the backbone of their sales message. And you would be wrong. THE single most perplexing aspect of selling I have ever seen.

The most powerful person on your sales team is your customer. Knowing that, why don't you take your customer with you on sales calls? They're better than you at closing the sale. Way better. Your customer, your cat AND your kids sell better than you. You are the WORST salesperson on your team.

Testimonial power secret. Most salespeople are so hell bent to get a testimonial, that they get the wrong kind, AND they fail to capture the most important element of a sale: Buying motives.

Asking a customer to tell you their reasons for purchasing from you will get you hundreds more sales of the same type.

Buying motives are 1,000 times more powerful than selling skills. Make that 10,000.

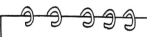

"THESE ARE THE BEST TESTIMONIALS WE COULD GET?"

TESTIMONIALS

What are your customers saying about you?

Principle 12

ANTENNAS UP!

- Using your 6th sense, the sense of selling.

Red R Bites

- What is your focus factor?
- "Antennas up" at all times.
- Awareness factor that's always around.
- The men's room at La Guardia airport.
- Flying to Dallas.

"I'M THE SALES FAIRY AND I'VE COME TO YOU WITH THREE WISHES ...
WORK YOUR ASS OFF, WORK YOUR ASS OFF, WORK YOUR ASS OFF!"

Using your 6th sense -- the sense of selling. Come to your senses -- your sales senses.

How do you sell? Many are untrained and go by their "gut feelings." Many say, "I just go about the process instinctively." Great – I hope you don't decide to switch and go into brain surgery.

The answer is using your "inside senses." If you're in control of these senses AND the dominant senses you radiate are positive, you can make sales – lots of them. The big question is: Do you radiate the positive senses or the negative ones?

Where do your inside senses come from? Your mind controls the senses that lead you to (sales) success. The positive senses lead to positive results. No brain surgery there.

Here are the 6 positive sales senses:

1. The sense of confidence – The air you have about you that's bred by preparation and previous wins. The best part about confidence is that it's contagious. You can give it to your prospect. (Don't confuse confidence with its evil twin – arrogance.)

2. The sense of positive anticipation – Everyone has read the best book on the subject before the age of five – *The Little Engine That Could*. I think I can, I think I can. Thinking you can is 50% of the outcome. (So is thinking you can't.)

3. The sense of determination – The sense of hanging in there no matter what. Determination is having the prospect tell you "no," and you hear it as, "not yet."

4. The sense of achievement – Everyone subconsciously strives for their goals. Sensing achievement comes from a replay of the satisfaction you gained from making your last sale. Remember how good it felt?

5. The sense of winning – Everyone wants to win, but only a few actually do. That's because the will to prepare to win must exceed the will to win.

6. The sense of success – This is the hardest sense to master, because you must sense it before you actually achieve it. That calm feeling of money in the bank. An "I can do it" attitude. And a well-lit path in front of you. The sense of positive purpose.

Pretty easy so far. But – the plot thickens. There are 8.5 negative senses that the subconscious mind presents and projects when selling:

1. The sense of fear.

2. The sense of nervousness.

3. The sense of rejection.

4. The sense of procrastination or reluctance.

5. The sense of justification/rationale.

6. The sense of self-doubt.

7. The sense of uncertainty.

8. The sense of doom.

8.5. The sense of "I'm unlucky."

Beware of these negative senses – they're mental blockers and will prevent the success (sale) from taking place.

The negative senses block your ability to focus on the positive senses – the creative ones that breed success. The most powerful way to get rid of the negatives is to counter-balance them with positive thoughts and words (ie: no complaining or blaming others).

Balancing by definition is delicate. Counter-balancing is even more so. It's a simultaneous act of chasing away negative senses, and focusing on the positive ones. It means harnessing and self-directing your inner thought process. Sounds simple, but it's not easy – that's why so few achieve greatness.

To further complicate things, you're not "sensing" alone. The prospect has senses too. And often he can sense your senses – especially the negative ones. If your negative senses like fear and self-doubt dominate your presentation, they will preoccupy the prospect. Result: The prospect will become nervous about you, and it will alter his ability to get a clear message. Make sense?

The great news about sales senses is, you're in total control. You can convert negative senses to positive senses with a combination of dedication to lifelong learning, and the achievement of a positive attitude. These studies will lead to taking positive actions.

Earl Nightingale, in his legendary tape, "The Strangest Secret," says, "You become what you think about." Truer words have never been spoken. But the secret to "The Strangest Secret," is – It's a dedicated self-discipline that must be practiced every day. How close to "every day" are you?

The most interesting aspect of "The Strangest Secret," is that it contains the counter balance to turn all your destructive senses into constructive senses by employing the strongest sense of them all – common sense.

Red  Bites

What is your focus-factor? Where is your attention? "Johnny, pay attention!" I'm certain that you heard those words a hundred times as you were growing up. All you have to do is substitute your name for Johnny's name. You thought you were being scolded. Actually you were being given one of life's most valuable lessons: Pay Attention! Now you're all grown up, and you still have not learned the lesson. You're more focused on yourself than you are on your world. Or should I say the world around you. When you're focused on yourself, (i.e., how you look, what you're wearing, what other people think of you) you are diverting your "focus energy" away from your success. Focus means intense purpose, and when you waste that focus on yourself, you're going to miss the opportunities around you. You're "out of focus." Everyone will tell you to focus or to BE more focused, but very few will tell you HOW to focus. The easiest words to describe "focus" are "be aware." Be aware of what is around you and be aware of who is around you. Sounds simple, but it means you have to divert selfish and insecure for open-minded and self-confident. The best way to explain this is to give you a couple of examples.

"Antennas up" at all times. My mentor and friend Earl Pertnoy has preached those words to me for more than twenty-five years. I don't care where you are: bathrooms, airport lines, lobbies of hotels, car washes, elevators, and restaurants are all ripe for making connections if you're alert. Follow Earl's advice as I do and you'll get the sales lead or the deal you were never expecting.

The awareness factor that's always around.
The "antennas up" philosophy starts with the awareness of your immediate surroundings. If you're looking to be a master seller, a large portion of that has to do with your understanding and your capitalization on where you are, who you meet, and what you say. If you're at an event, your job is to keep your antennas up until you meet the key players regardless of what it takes. You may have to ask someone, "where's the big cheese?" You may have to look at every name tag. You may have to stay until everyone has left. You may even have to stand next to the person until the conversation that they're having with someone else is completed. But if you're antennas are somewhere in a bottle of beer, or with your friends, or looking for more food, the odds are that they're pointed in the wrong direction. And not only will you not win, you will lose to someone whose antennas are pointed in the right direction.

True story: The men's room at LaGuardia Airport –
I got off the plane and had to use the facilities. The
men's rooms at LaGuardia are full of urinals. You must also
understand the rule of men's rooms: men don't talk. They pee,
they wash their hands, and then they leave. I happen to glance
to the left of me and saw Hal Linden (a.k.a. Barney Miller)
and said (as we were peeing), "The great equalizer of men."
He started to howl. He almost peed on his shoes, which by the
way were Hush Puppies. I asked, "Goin' into the city?" He said,
"Yep." I said, "wanna split a cab?" He said, "sure." And we drove
into the city through the Astoria district of Queens where
Archie Bunker lived and the Barney Miller police station was
located. It was a great ride. When we got to the city, he paid
for the whole thing. My antennas were up. I had the guts to
make the exchange, and I won. Did I win big? No, but I had
fun. In the game of antennas up, it's not always about winning
big. It's about having a good time, and it's about practice. I
never fail to keep my antennas up, and I never fail to capitalize
on the opportunity when it occurs. Neither should you.

True Story: Flying to Dallas. The other day I was flying
from Buffalo to Dallas. As usual, my antennas were up. Sitting
next to me on the plane was Hall of Fame quarterback Jim
Kelly. We chatted a bit, but I certainly didn't want to bring up
the words "Super Bowl." So I began to tell him that I was an
author and a speaker, and that I had actually been on the same
program with him a couple of times and had a couple of his
autographed footballs. He smiled. I said, "As a noted speaker
and an author, you probably want my autograph." So I
autographed my boarding card and handed it to him. He sat
there kind of dumb-founded, and after about 30 seconds I said,

"I wouldn't mind if you autographed yours and gave it to me."
He laughed, autographed his boarding pass, and handed both
of them back to me. It was fun.

It's important for you to understand that focus and selling
yourself are not about tactics. Selling is not about techniques.
Selling is about focus and creative verbal exchange. And the
only way to master focus is to work at it.

Antennas up?
Antennas up!

Principle 12.5

RESIGN YOUR POSITION AS GENERAL MANAGER OF THE UNIVERSE

"I KNOW EVERYONE IS ALL SCREWED UP, EXCEPT FOR ME!"

You now have all the principles necessary for your success as a salesperson. Your ass is kicked, you're prepared to win, your brand is known, you sell on value, you're face to face, you talk to the decision maker, you're engaging, you're funny, you're creative, you've reduced their risk, you use testimonials to complete the transaction, and your antennas are up.

But there's more. You need glue. You need to understand how to make each of these principles your own. You have to master these principles.

And the first part of that is to master yourself. Most people are caught up in other people's drama. Did Bill Clinton lie? Did O.J. Simpson kill her? Did Kobe Bryant rape her? Will Ben marry J. Lo? Answer: Who cares? Better answer: How do any of these events affect your life? Best answer: They don't. Yet you will spend tens maybe hundreds of hours focused on this crap at the expense of your own career and your own success. Let's get closer to home.

You have a boss, you have a team of salespeople, you have customers, maybe vendors, you have friends, and they all have lives, problems, and situations.

Stay out of them.

Every time you stick your nose in somebody else's business you risk 3.5 things.

1. Joining their pity party further promulgating their situation

2. Giving bad advice

3. Wasting your own time that could be spent learning, making sales, and earning

3.5 Getting your nose punched

If you add up the time you spend where it's none of your business, or none of your concern, or that you cannot affect the outcome (news, TV reruns, and other crap) you could have been the greatest salesperson in the world or a syndicated columnist, or an author. But no, you'd rather piss your time down the drain thinking that you're some kind of savior to mankind when in fact, it's just the opposite. Save your own ass first.

When you have mastered your own self-discipline … When you have mastered the science of selling … When you have mastered your personal positive attitude forever … When you have mastered becoming a dynamic presenter … When you have mastered your own financial affairs … When you have mastered your own family life … When you have mastered your own personal life, then and only then should you begin thinking about putting your nose in somebody else's affairs.

Now I know, this seems a bit harsh, and at the end of a book you tend to want everyone to live happily ever after and have the package tied up in some neat bow.

That's not what I want.

What I want is for you to go back to the beginning of the book and use this last chapter as impetus and incentive to implement the first principle, Kick Your Own Ass. It's a cycle. A sales cycle. Your sales cycle.

In 1972, when the twins were born, I was in a rotten marriage, I was broke, and I was studying positive attitude daily. I first read the phrase *resign your position as general manager of the universe*. I have searched back and cannot find its origin. I wish I could. I wish I could tell you that I created this phrase, but I can't. What I can tell you is that I have used this philosophy as one of the building blocks to my success. The reason that I have saved it for last is because it is the least evident and the most difficult.

Everyone violates the principle *resign your position as general manger of the universe.* Even me. The difference between you and me is I violate it less than you do. People come to me all the time because I am so good at sales, they think I am also good at life, and will often ask me to help resolve a "situation." The only two things I do are tell them are my personal experiences, and issue them the three word challenge: Seek professional help. I'm not a psychologist, I'm not a psychiatrist, I'm certainly not a marriage counselor, I'm just a salesman and a dad (not in that order).

RED WHINE ...

"I'm surrounded by a bunch of people with lousy ..."

The closest thing I come to advice with respect to a question I often get, "What should I do with my career?" or "Should I find another job?" or "What kind of sales position should I take?" Those are big questions. Those are life questions. I'm not going to give someone a specific answer what to do. First of all it lets them off the hook, and second of all I don't want to impose my will on theirs. I'm persuasive and to many I'm influential. That's

not a fair fight. The advice I give them is the same advice I'd give you. Find something that you love, find something that you can believe in, find an environment that's fun, and people you can respect and jump in with both feet.

That's as close as I get to someone else's universe. And you need to do the same thing if you want to achieve any level of success in your personal career.

The reason I have asked you to "resign" is that you are already in the middle of a hundred things where you can not affect the outcome or worse, may even be blamed for the outcome. Get the hell out of that as fast as you can. Lock your doors, turn on a light, grab a book and a highlighter and start to read.

If you convert the time that you are currently spending in someone else's universe to your own universe, in less than five years you can be king of your universe. When you achieve the status of king you can again begin to hold court. But my bet is you won't want to.

Resigning your position as general manager of the universe is the single best step you can take to buying back the time that you claim you don't have, and give yourself a new opportunity to achieve at a level that

RED SELLING RESPONSE ...
"I finally got rid of everything with the word lousy in it, including the people attached to it. Now I'm concentrating on making my life perfect (and boy do I have a long way to go)."

here-to-fore you have only dreamed about, and were not able to achieve.

The minute you decide to resign is the same minute that you have chosen a smoother road to personal success.

Your choice.

The less time you spend in other people's business, other people's problems, and other people's drama, the more time you'll have for your own success.

– Jeffrey Gitomer

Some more RED formulas you can use to succeed ...

Now that you have read the principles, there are still some guidelines that you must *understand* in order to master the principles. In the pages that follow you will get a better mental picture of what you, the salesperson, must do in order to take the principles that you have read and turn them into money.

Turn the page ...

I think I can. I think I can.
I thought I could. I thought I could.
The little salesman that could.
A story. A philosophy. A strategy. A formula. A win. A BIG win.

I've had more than 50 birthdays. And let's just say that they're not as exciting to me as they once were. However, they are more stimulating. More thought provoking. And with each passing one, more intense. I think there is an old saying that goes, "The flame burns brightest near the end." And not that I feel I am near the end, but I certainly feel the flame burning brighter.

I started to think of my favorite books. And for more than fifty years, my favorite book has been, *The Little Engine That Could*. It's all about a train trying to make it up a hill. Others tried to discourage her, but she had enough fan support, enough cheerleaders, to make it up the hill using the timeless phrase, "I think I can, I think I can."

Well, naturally my thoughts turned to sales. And why not revive this 1930 classic with my version of The Little Salesman that Could. And what started out to be a whimsical thought ended up being a seminar at the Charlotte Home Builders Association.

I will try my best to re-create the points of the seminar. I think I can. I think I can.

In order for salespeople to make it "up the hill" they must have
the same qualities as that 73-year-old little engine. And please
keep in mind that for every little engine that could, there are
a hundred or more that couldn't.

Interesting to note that no one ever wrote a book about the
little engine that couldn't. Also interesting to note that in 1930
the author, Watty Piper, had the foresight to make the little
engine a heroine rather than a hero.

Here are elements that I challenge you to think about and
self-evaluate in your little engine. These are not "how to" sales
techniques. Rather, they are "why I" elements of personal
development. They are not "sales now," they are "sales forever."
They are not about commissions. They are about wealth. And
not just monetary wealth. They are also wealth of knowledge.

1. Your total belief system. The theme of the book is also
the theme of your success. Believing that you can achieve
whatever you set your mind to. You must believe that you
work for the greatest company in the world, that you offer the
greatest products and services in the world, and that you are
the greatest person in the world, or you are in the wrong job.
High self-belief leads to high success. Medium self-belief leads
to medium success. Low self-belief … you get the idea.

2. Belief drives passion. Mediocrity stems from lack of
belief more than lack of skill. Passion is the intangible in a
salesperson's presentation that makes the message transferable.
Passion exhibited by the salesperson creates a desire to buy in
the heart and mind of the prospect. Passion exhibited by the
salesperson converts selling to buying. (People don't like to be
sold, but they love to buy.) It's an emotional transfer that can
later be justified logically.

3. Have the attitude of YES! I think I can is a "yes" thought, not just a positive thought. It is a positive determination with a positive projected outcome. It is more than determination. It's YES. A "yes" attitude is stated in terms of what can be done and stated of a positive outcome. Earl Nightingale, in his legendary recording, "The Strangest Secret" says: "You become what you think about all day long." Think you can.

4. Invest your time in things that will help you succeed. How many hours a day do you spend in 'non-success' areas? Time wasters like TV re-runs, news for the second time today, or someone else's drama. What could you achieve if you took half of that time and invested it in studying about your biggest business obstacle or biggest business opportunity? Suppose you just decided to become an expert in relationship building. An hour a day will make you a world class expert in five years. Or you can take that same hour and become a world class expert in re-runs of ER. The choice is yours, and those who will pass you. Think you can stop watching so much TV.

5. Begin capturing your thoughts, strategies and ideas in writing. If someone were to ask me for ONE thing that I can pinpoint to my success, without a nanosecond of hesitation, I would answer, "writing." In a month, I will enter my thirteenth year of writing this column. Success is a low level word when I describe what the discipline of writing has done for my career, my success, my fulfillment, and my legacy. It should also be noted that I never started out to be "a writer." I was merely clarifying my thoughts about my strategies, philosophies, and methods of selling, and then getting them published. I never wrote a book, I just wrote a column. However, the column has turned into three books. If you only choose to believe ONE THING that I tell you: Believe that

writing will take you from where you are to any place you
want to go. Think you can write.

6. Take a course in writing. Learning how to write will
help you put words you are thinking about into clear, concise,
written thoughts and ideas. Personally I have found the more
I write, the more ideas I get, and the clearer they become.
Most people think, "I can't write" or "I am not a good writer."
Easy answer. Study writing. Read someone whose writing you
like. Write your thoughts down. Take a course in writing.
And then begin to refine your technique or style. When I first
began writing I thought I was a pretty good writer. I just
re-read my first ten columns. They pretty much sucked.
But, I thought I could, I did, I learned, and then I refined.

NOTE WELL: I wish there was a way I could explain the
power of the written word. The only thing I can say is to
re-enforce my earlier statement that every piece of business
good fortune for the last 13 years has in some way or another
come from writing.

7. Take a course in something you love. By learning more
about what you love to do, it will create a positive atmosphere
and a positive mindset about learning and achieving. The
things you love to do, you do with passion. The combination
of learning, achieving, and passion can make for world class
expertise in anything you think you can.

**8. Get so Internet savvy that you can teach a 14-year-old
rather than vice-versa.** Many adult business people are
functional computer illiterates. If you don't have your own
website, and you don't have your own e-mail address, and you
don't access the Internet every day, and you think you are in

the business world, think again. People who did not grow up in the computer age may have let it pass them by. It's OK, it's OK. Not everyone thought automobiles would make it either. Some people thought radios were stupid. And someone in their infinite wisdom thought there would only be a market for two dozen laptops (this statement was made after extensive research). I believe that person is now a waiter at Shoney's. If you are at the crossroads of Internet entry and computer literacy, I implore you to think you can. Computers are cheap, Internet access is cheaper, and both are 21st century tools that are the gateway to your fame, fortune, financial freedom, fulfillment, and fun.

9. Begin clarifying your ideas in public – and get known as a person of value at the same time. After I began writing, people began to call and ask if I would speak at their civic organization (Rotary, Kiwanis). It gave me a chance to speak and listen to my written thoughts. Speaking, like writing, is a barrier to entry in the world of success. Rather than taking a course in speaking, you only have to join Toastmasters. Live speaking opportunities from the first meeting (toastmasters.org). Speaking strikes fear in the heart of the unprepared. But, speaking will position you as a leader and a thinker in your community or your industry.

NOTE WELL: If you write your thoughts down, speaking becomes infinitely more simple. Once you get past a little bit of fear, it's not only fun, it's profitable. It's also an open door (and an open wallet) to anyone in your audience. If they like you, it's likely that they will pay to see you again.

10. Publish something. This column is my words of advice published by someone else. Being published has an authenticity about it. The written word is very authoritative and is often tantamount to believability ('Dewey wins!' not withstanding). Being published also means that someone believes your thoughts are worthy enough or sound enough for others to read. It's an affirmation that your thinking is clear and your direction is sound. It is one of the ultimate "I think I can-I thought I could," achievements.

10.5. Give value first. This is a philosophy and a strategy that I learned by accident, that has become the key differentiator between how others "sell" while I create the atmosphere to "buy." Here is the marketing strategy (another accident) that arose from that philosophy: "I put myself in front of people who can say 'yes' to me, and I deliver value first." The overused and baseless expression "added-value" or its brother "value-added," means you have to buy first in order to receive any value. It's referred to as an incentive. My take on it is that it's somewhere between silly, non-existent, self-serving, or begging.

My strategy (and soon to be a book) is to put valuable information in the hands of my most probable purchasers so that they may benefit, get to know me, come to respect me, and then call me wanting to purchase. This is not a theory, it's a strategy that has been working for thirteen years. It is important to note that this strategy was not, "I think I can, it just happened as a result of all the other "I think I can's." It's an "I thought I could." It was the classic case of cause and effect rather than preconceived notion.

Well, there's the formula. Think you can? Or do you think it sounds like too much work? Why don't you not pre-judge what is hard or easy, and begin by purchasing (or going to your kids bedroom and getting) a copy of *The Little Engine That Could*. That's an easy way to start your thinking process. I know, it sounds simplistic, almost hokey, but so does every other self-help book ever written. Hokey but accurate.

I have just given you a birthday present on my birthday. I am going to add a wish. I wish you would take this information and read it three or four times. And I wish you would take action in some way that might begin to put you on a better path to achievement, success, and fulfillment.

If you know me, you know that I very rarely wish for anything. Maybe because I believe wishing is a poor substitute for hard work. I can wish all I want, but the hard work is up to you. And my feeling about it is, of course, I think you can. I think you can.

The two most important words in selling. Two words that define sales … Your sales.

Can you guess what they are? Make money, customer service, close sales, follow-up. No. They're words about sales – I'm talking about two words that lead to sales. Hint: The words are separate.

Give up? The first word is you. Many salespeople believe that customers buy their products and services first. Incorrect. The first thing prospects buy is the salesperson. The first sale made is you.

In order to affect any direct sale the customer must first believe in the person conveying the message. This is unfortunately most evident when "you" is bad. Ever walk out of a car dealership because the salesperson was too pushy, or worse, insulted you? Then drove somewhere else and bought the same product because they were "nice" to you. You bought the salesperson – then you bought the product.

Ever had a rude salesperson or server, and walked away without purchasing? Not only did you walk away, you told friends and associates the horror story. The person couldn't sell themselves, therefore couldn't complete a sale that the customer was anxious to make. Amazing isn't it?

It all begins with you. Prospects must first believe in (and like) the messenger, or the message has no credibility.

How's your personal product? How's your you? Is it salable – or does it need some work?

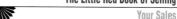

Rate your *you*. Here are 10.5 things that make "you" strong enough to make a sale. Rate yourself in each category from one (poor) to ten (the greatest) – and see how great "you" are. Put your rating in the box.

☐ **1. Your image.** How you look affects the way you are perceived. How do you look?

☐ **2. Your ability to speak.** Your ability to convey the message. Are you a member of toastmasters?

☐ **3. Your ability to establish rapport.** Making the prospect feel at ease, and developing some common ground as a basis to move forward. Do you make the scene warm?

☐ **4. Your attitude.** Your enthusiasm combined with your state of internal happiness. Not what you say, but how you say it. Are you positive plus?

☐ **5. Your product knowledge.** Your convincability. Do you know it cold?

☐ **6. Your desire to help.** Desire to help shows through, so does greed. Does your help side outweigh your greed side?

☐ **7. Your preparedness.** A confidence builder if you are, or destroyer if you aren't. Do you prepare for every call?

☐ **8. Your humor.** Nothing builds good feelings like good humor and a good laugh. Can you make others laugh?

☐ **9. Your creativity.** What separates you from your competition? How do you make followups that don't just beg for the sale? What makes them talk about you? Your creativity – How's yours?

☐ **10. Your sincerity.** Shows through either way. Are you genuine?

☐ **11. Your reputation** (or the reputation that precedes you). If you are well known in the community, or in your field, you may walk in with a slight advantage. How's your reputation?

☐ **11.5 Your glue.** The way you handle your total package. Your Stature. The way you carry yourself. The way you put it all together. The character of you is what leads to the credibility of what you sell. How well are you "put together"?

How'd you score? Perfect score is 120. If you scored from 110-120, you are a great "you," with a great success story to tell, and are setting a great example for others.

99-109 Pretty darn good you. Climbing the ladder, and making daily progress.

70-98 You ain't as hot as you think. You're in need of a 20-minute personal daily workout.

50-69 You're mediocre at sales, and so is your success to date. You have a decision to make. Stay and get better every day, or get out before you're fired, and blame someone else for all that's wrong with you.

30-49 You stink. Go to the nearest bookstore, buy Dale Carnegie's *How to Win Friends and Influence People*. Don't leave home until you read it.

Making *you* great is fun. And it will make more sales than 1,000 sales techniques. Oh, and for those of you who have a long way to go, here's the best advice I've ever heard to start (and stay) on the path to being the best – You are the greatest, if you think you are.

The second most important word in selling is *why*. It's important because it leads to the one thing you can't make sales without – answers.

The word why applies to three aspects of your sales (and your) life:

Why you?
Why them?
Why ask?

Why you: Why are you in sales? To make "good" money? False. A better (and more truthful) answer is what you will do with the money. What your money will buy you. Who you will help with your money. That's your real why.

Determining the real reason why you're in sales will allow you to go into a sales call with a purpose – a mission. Identifying and developing your "why" will help you achieve the dedication and self-discipline you need to learn to become a great salesperson. Discovery of "why" will also lead you to the belief that you are the best.

Self-belief is the first and most critical function of the selling process. How's yours?

Success strategy: Write your *"why"* in a few words (example: "I want my son to go to the college of his choice.") on 3"x 5" cards and place them in five strategic locations.

1. On your bathroom mirror.

2. On the dashboard of your car.

3. On the wall of your office where you can see it (maybe on your computer).

4. On your office telephone.

5. In your wallet (near your money).

You may have more than one why – for best results, post them all.

Why them: The biggest mistake salespeople make is trying to sell for the wrong reasons – their own. You see, people don't buy for your reasons – they buy for *their* reasons – so find their reasons (their "why") first and sell them on that.

Finding out the prospect's real *"why"* is the most important process of the selling process.

Success strategy: The real *why* you're after may be 3 or 4 questions deep. When you get a superficial why answer, ask why again. It will get you closer to the real truth.

Secrets to the discovery of "why":

• People may be embarrassed or reluctant to reveal their real *why*.

• People may not know their real *why* because they never

thought about it (had the guts to think about it, had the courage to face it).

• The real *why* may be behind the stated need. Something they really need to accomplish, something they hate, love, or are passionate about.

• The real *why* only comes to the surface with the proper use of part three:

Why ask: Questions are the heart of sales. To get the true *why* of the prospect, you must ask the right why questions. Questions that get the prospect to answer about your desires stated in their interests or needs. Ask them questions about them (their *why*), and have *them* answer in terms of *you* (your *why*).

Why is the questioning element of the sale that will lead to other pathways of information – if asked properly.

Why leads you to all the answers you need in order complete a sale, define expectations, and build a relationship.

Why gets down to the real reasons for the sale – yours and theirs.

Success strategy: Pre-plan your questions. Have a list with you to refer to at all times. Test them out for reaction and their ability to generate response.

The two most important words in sales – *you* and *why* – are part of a formula that every salesperson should have emblazoned on their soul: *you* + *why* = *yes!*

> *"The biggest reason people don't succeed
> is because they don't expose themselves
> to existing information."*
>
> – Jim Rohn, America's business philosopher

12.5 Principles of Life-long Learning

Rate yourself in the box on the left of each principle.
(1=poor, 2=average, 3=good, 4=very good, 5=the greatest)
(1=never, 2=rarely, 3=sometimes, 4=frequently, 5=always)

☐ **1. It Starts with a positive attitude** … Learn how to
achieve one. Gather the information of positive people
in your library.

Napoleon Hill	Dale Carnegie	W. Clement Stone
Maxwell Maltz	Wayne Dyer	Earl Nightengale
Norman Vincent Peale	Jim Rohn	

☐ **2. Listen to audio tapes** – Own several sets and play
them in your car.

☐ **3. Read books** – Build your library one (read) book
a month.

☐ **4. Attend live seminars** – as many as you can afford,
as often as you can.

STAY A STUDENT ...

"If you want to be wealthy study wealth and hang around wealthy people. The same goes for if you want to be a great salesperson, or if you want to be a great comedian, or if you want to be a great dad. The element of student, the element of mentor, the element of attitude, and the element of selfish all play a vital role in this process."

☐ **5.** **Join Toastmasters** – 90 minutes of speaking and self-evaluation a week.

☐ **6.** **Record yourself speaking** – a weekly ritual.

☐ **7.** **Record yourself reading** – a weekly ritual.

☐ **8.** **Record yourself selling** – a weekly ritual.

☐ **9.** **Record your personal commercial** – a weekly ritual.

☐ **10.** **Record your own set of sales tapes** – Get great at selling and presenting at the same time.

☐ **11.** **Listen to your own tapes as much as you listen to others.**

☐ **12.** **Spend 30 minutes a day learning something new.**

☐ **12.5** **Practice what you've learned as soon as you learn it.**

Score:

65-70 = WOW!

59-64 = AOK

21-58 = Get help!

0-20 = Start (your life) over

Implement the Rule of "The More, The More"

Love it or leave it. The more you love it, the more you will sell.
The more you prepare for the sale, the more you will sell. The
more you believe it, the more you will sell. If your self-belief
isn't sky high, why bother?

The *More* you watch TV, the *More* the competition will kick your ass.

What does it take to be number one? And stay there!

I called Bob Higgins, southeast regional sales director for Cintas (The Uniform People) and asked to interview his BEST salesperson. "Jeffrey, that's easy," Bob said with pride. "The Southeast's best salesperson is also the company's best salesperson, and she has been the past three years. Her name is Terri Norris."

I asked Bob to ask Terri to e-mail me her ten best qualities. The ones she felt "put her over the top." The e-mail arrived the next morning (no surprise) and it began like this: "Hello Jeffrey! When Bob Higgins asked me to call you with my 'top 10 best qualities' I said, "What! Only 10?" Well, if I can ONLY give you 10, here they are …"

Spoken with the personal pride and self-confidence of a "number one." All salespeople are different with one exception – they all want to make the sale. So as you read this list, be advised that these qualities may not be the ones you seek to attain or master. That's up to you. They are presented to you because Atlanta-based Terri Norris is the number one salesperson on a team of more than a thousand, and she didn't get there by accident. So I thought you might be interested in how a winner thinks and acts.

Here, in her own words, are the top ten qualities and characteristics of what makes Terri Norris number one.

1. A contagious positive attitude. I believe that I am blessed and that positive things will happen in my life. Because I believe that positive things will happen to me, they do!

2. Excited about the prospect of helping others. Sincerely caring. When I have appointments, I want to help my prospective customers solve a problem, get better service, increase productivity, etc. I believe that they can sense that I want to help them and not "sell them something."

3. Self-assured, not arrogant. Confidence. I know that I can achieve whatever I decide to and am willing to work hard for. I believe in myself and my abilities. My personal motto is "They can, who believe they can. I believe I can."

4. I like people and they like me. People like me right away. I'm not a threat to them. And I'm not perceived as "salesy." Being able to relate to people, ALL people. I don't try to "type" people; I just try to "like" them.

5. Not just "book smart." Being able to assess and solve real-world problems. Being able to prioritize and decide which things (prospects) to spend time on and which not to. Work smarter, not harder.

6. If I'm not having fun, what's the point? I have often been described as "easily amused." I think this is one of my best characteristics. I find joy in almost everything.

7. I do everything full-force. I sweat when I work and I sweat when I dance. 110% is the minimum acceptable standard. If something is worthwhile, I give it everything I have.

8. Unspoken integrity. Visibly honest. I try to be honest and ethical in everything that I do. I feel that being trustworthy and honorable is a strong statement of character. I try to always keep my promises. Hopefully, my word means something to others, because it means EVERYTHING to me.

9. I concentrate on the details without getting caught up in them. Beyond organized. Detail is vital to my success. It sounds minute, but it's HUGE. I keep things in order so I can function error-free. I try not to waste time or energy by trying to find things twice or pick up dropped balls.

10. I'm kid-like happy on the inside. I have the enthusiasm of a 2-year-old with a college degree and a business card. I am the eternal cheerleader for myself and others. I want everyone to win (except my competition).

I interviewed Terri at the Cintas Southeast sales conference. Besides being a gem of a person, her interview produced several verbal gems – here are a few more for your thought-enjoyment.

• My attitude knob is always set on positive.

• I create rapport so that the prospect feels like he or she is in my home and can go to my fridge and get a Coca-Cola (or Diet Coke, my favorite) without asking.

Then I asked her if there was any one characteristic she'd place over the others? "I am Gomer Pyle friendly, sincere, and believable." She said that with pride.

Well gohleeee! No wonder she's number one.

Free Red **Bit:** Want some more number one wisdom? I've prepared a list of Terri Norris' sales gems and philosophies from our interview. Winning philosophies and strategies. Want them? Go to www.gitomer.com, register if you are a first time user, and enter the word NORRIS in the RedBit box.

Some of you are
reading this and saying,
"Jeffrey, don't bug me
with this philosophy stuff,
tell me how to make sales."

I am.

This is the most powerful sales
lesson I can deliver.

Only a few will get it –
**the ones who will
rise to the top**.

This Book Has No Ending ...

You have not reached the end of the book. You have reached the end of your first reading of the book. *The Little Red Book of Selling* is not something that you read and put on the shelf. *The Little Red Book of Selling* is to be read and re-read. That's why I put **RED** in the title.

If you hear a song on the radio and you like it, you want to hear it again. If you hear it five times you can sing along. If you hear it ten times you can sing it on your own. It's the same with this book. If you want to be the master ten times is the key.

When I first studied attitude Napoleon Hill's *Think and Grow Rich* was our bible. We had to read one chapter each day. Since there are only 15 chapters it meant that every three weeks we completed the book. I did this for one year. Read the book approximately 15 times. Actually I didn't read the book, I owned the book. And it was my guiding light towards a permanent positive attitude. Was that a dumb thing to do? I don't know, my friends at the time thought it was. They still have negative attitudes.

This is not a book to be read, this is a book to be studied. This is a book to be implemented. This is a book to be talked about. This is a book to be put into your sales life. There's too much content in here for you to read it once and put it away and say good read. If you read it ten times it will be great sales, great attitude, great creativity, great relationships, great bank account, great life.

If you have not
mastered every
red principle,
go back and study
each one.
If you have not
mastered every
red principle,
go back and
make a game plan
for each one.
If you have not
mastered every
red principle,
go forward and
implement each one.

Jeffrey Gitomer
Chief Executive Salesman

Author. Jeffrey Gitomer is the author of *The Sales Bible* now in its 18th printing, and *Customer Satisfaction Is Worthless - Customer Loyalty Is Priceless*. Jeffrey's books have sold more than 500,000 copies worldwide.

Over 100 presentations a year. Jeffrey gives seminars, runs annual sales meetings, and conducts training programs on selling and customer service. He has presented an average of 115 seminars a year for the past 10 years.

Photograph by Mitchell Kearney

Big Corporate Customers. Jeffrey's customers include Coca-Cola, Cingular Wireless, Hilton, Choice Hotels, Enterprise Rent-A-Car, Cintas, Milliken, NCR, Financial Times, Turner Broadcasting, Comcast Cable, Time Warner Cable, HBO, Ingram Micro, Wells Fargo Bank, BMW, Baptist Health Care, Blue Cross Blue Shield, Hyatt Hotels, Carlsburg Beer, Wausau Insurance, Northwestern Mutual, Sports Authority, GlaxoSmithKline, XEROX, A.C. Nielsen, Ricoh U.S., AT&T, and hundreds of others.

In front of millions of readers every week. His syndicated column Sales Moves appears in more than 90 business newspapers, and is read by more than 3,500,000 people every week.

And every month. Jeffrey's column appears in more than 25 trade publications and newsletters. Jeffrey has also been a contributor and featured expert in *Entrepreneur* and *Selling Power* magazines.

On the Internet. His three WOW websites – *www.gitomer.com*, *www.trainone.com*, and *www.knowsuccess.com* get as many as 5,000 hits a day from readers and seminar attendees. His state of the art web-presence and e-commerce ability has set the standard among peers, and has won huge praise and acceptance from customers.

Up Your Sales Web-based Sales Training. A weekly streaming video (low cost – high value) sales training lesson is now available on *www.trainone.com*. The content is pure Jeffrey – fun, pragmatic, real world, and immediately implementable. This innovation is leading the way in the field of e-learning.

Sales Caffeine. A weekly "e-zine" sales wake-up call delivered every Tuesday morning to more than 100,000 subscribers free of charge. This allows us to communicate valuable sales information, strategies, and answers to sales professionals on a timely basis.

Sales Assessment Online. New for 2003, is the world's first customized sales assessment. Renamed a "successment," this amazing sales tool will not only judge your selling skill level in twelve critical areas of sales knowledge, it will give you a diagnostic report that includes 50 mini sales lessons as it rates your sales abilities, and explains your customized opportunities for sales knowledge growth. Aptly named KnowSuccess – the company's mission is: *You can't know success until you know yourself.*

Award for Presentation Excellence. In 1997, Jeffrey was awarded the designation Certified Speaking Professional (CSP) by the National Speakers Association. The CSP award has been given less than 500 times in the past 25 years.

BuyGitomer, Inc.
310 Arlington Avenue • Loft 329
Charlotte, N.C. 28203
www.gitomer.com • 704.333.1112 • www.trainone.com
salesman@gitomer.com

Acknowledgments and Thanks

To **Ray Bard** for his great idea, excellent persistence, and total support along the way. The words 'honest publisher' are very rare to find in combination. But in the dictionary it would say, see also Ray Bard.

To **Mike Sakoonserksadee** for the cover design. It looks simple, but we went through about fifty versions before we settled on the right type, the right size, and the right placement. Michael has patience, and an eye for what works.

To **Dave Pinski** for the spiral art cityscape. Dave hit it on the first draw and with just a few modifications has created the ultimate definition of a salesperson. Ups and downs in the never ending spiral staircase in the forefront of the city where nothing happens until a sale is made.

To **Rachel Russotto** for the hard work and editing done on this book – the BEST. Actually Rachel is not an editor, she's a blessing.

To **Greg Russell** for great graphic design, for hard work at odd hours, for instant response, and overall excellence in taste and performance. You are now officially a member of the Gitomer family (healthcare not included).

To **Teresa Gitomer**, for understanding that just because I'm in work zone doesn't mean I don't love her. In success, support is everything. Thank you.

For absent people who continue to provide inspiration from heaven. In the never ending loving memory of Max and Florence Gitomer.

If you make a sale,
you can earn
a commission.

If you make a friend,
you can earn
a fortune.

– Jeffrey Gitomer

Turn the RED into GREEN.

The Little Red Book of Selling is available
as a blended learning solution.
This will enable you and your organization
to take these 12.5 principles of sales greatness
and make them come alive in your company.

The Little Red Book of Selling
packaged training contains:
facilitator guides, participant workbooks,
mulit-media support, job aides,
and e-learning reinforcement.

Call 704.333.1112 and scream, "More Red!"

Other Titles by Jeffrey Gitomer

**Customer Satisfaction Is Worthless,
Customer Loyalty Is Priceless:
How to Make Customers *Love* You,
Keep Them Coming Back and
Tell *Everyone* They Know**
(Bard Press, 1998)

**The Sales Bible:
The Ultimate Sales Resource**
(Wiley & Sons, 2003)

The Patterson Principles of Selling
(Wiley & Sons, 2004)

**Wrestling With Success:
Developing a Championship Mentality**;
Jeffrey Gitomer and Nikita Koloff
(Wiley & Sons, 2004)

Knock Your Socks Off Selling;
Jeffrey Gitomer and Ron Zemke
(Amacom, 1999)